THE OBAMA MOVEMENT

THE OBAMA MOVEMENT

✦

Why Barack Obama Speaks to America's Youth

Compiled by

JOSEPH VOGEL

Author of *Free Speech 101*

iUniverse, Inc.

New York Lincoln Shanghai

THE OBAMA MOVEMENT
Why Barack Obama Speaks
to America's Youth

iUniverse books may be ordered through booksellers or by contacting:

iUniverse
2021 Pine Lake Road, Suite 100
Lincoln, NE 68512
www.iuniverse.com
1-800-Authors (1-800-288-4677)

Because of the dynamic nature of the Internet, any Web addresses or links contained in this book may have changed since publication and may no longer be valid.

The views expressed in this work are solely those of the author and do not necessarily reflect the views of the publisher, and the publisher hereby disclaims any responsibility for them.

ISBN: 978-0-595-46703-7 (pbk)
ISBN: 978-0-595-90999-5 (ebk)

Printed in the United States of America

"Every generation needs a new revolution."

—Thomas Jefferson

Contents

ACKNOWLEDGMENTS

I express my sincere gratitude to everyone who has contributed to this project. Your individual stories have combined to create a powerful statement against the idea that young people don't care about politics.

A special thanks to the Obama campaign for your insight and support; to Michael Larsen and the Larsen-Pomada Literary Agency for your efforts and encouragement; to Kristine Deku, for your advice, feedback, and assistance from the beginning; and to Stephen McIntyre, for superb editing and revisions.

Finally, to my wife Tiffany, and yet to be born baby: You're the inspiration for everything.

INTRODUCTION

I woke up early the day of Senator Barack Obama's presidential announcement. Like thousands of other young people across the country, I had suddenly been re-engaged in politics. Perhaps the more appropriate term would be *engaged* since there had never been a politician in my lifetime that made the night before a political announcement seem exciting.

Sure, I voted in previous elections, I watched the debates, and read *Newsweek*. But the idea of actually participating in a campaign never even crossed my mind. The world of politics seemed, for the most part, like a distant charade, a game, a celebration of corruption and compromise. I cared about my community, my state, my country, and the world, and in fact, was eager to make a difference, but I felt politics was the last way to affect real change.

And now, within months, it was a whole different story. I had signed up as a volunteer for the Obama campaign, I had donated money, I had driven six hours to Las Vegas with my wife to listen to a stump speech; I had even inexplicably started a grassroots organization online called Barack the Youth Vote in the middle of a semester of graduate school that grew into the thousands within a few weeks. Emails came pouring in from people all over the country. People were anxious to get involved.

This basic narrative I have described—of being awakened and engaged in the political process for the first time—is only unique in its details. Its sentiment is heard over and over among young supporters of Barack Obama. Each has a story of transformation—of action replacing apathy, of interest replacing disillusionment, of hope replacing cynicism.

Individually, they might not seem that significant; collectively they reveal a movement.

◆ ◆ ◆

My personal transformation requires a bit of background. In the fall of 2004, I experienced the ugliness of politics in a very personal way. As student vice president of academics at my college, I decided to invite film maker Michael Moore to speak at our school which was situated in Utah County, one of the most conservative communities in the country. The goal was to energize our campus and community, to get students exploring and thinking about issues that mattered, and ultimately to vote. I personally wasn't enthused about either Bush or Kerry; politically, I was an independent. But I still felt with the war raging on, with the gap continuing to widen between the rich and the poor, and with unprecedented threats on our civil liberties, it was important for young people to be informed and to care.

In response to this speaking invitation to Michael Moore came fury like I could have never imagined. There were thousands of phone calls, emails, and letters. People said I had betrayed my faith, my country, and my family. Wealthy donors to the college tried to bribe us to cancel with tens of thousands of dollars. State legislators threatened to withhold badly needed funding for the college. A lawsuit was filed against us by a local community member. Even Fox News's Sean Hannity was invited to come and speak in a purported effort to "balance" the speech by Moore.

In the midst of the madness, there were some encouraging signs: we had our highest student voter registration ever, some people practiced civility and engaged in serious and open-minded dialogue; and after weeks of standing up against the threats and bribes and hate mail, free speech eventually prevailed as the people of Utah were able to listen to an unpopular, minority view.

Unfortunately, however, in many ways the spectacle mirrored what was taking place all across America. Those with dissenting views were called "anti-American," while all conservatives were labeled ignorant bigots. On both sides, I saw hate, rage, hysteria, and fear. I saw people band together for various causes, each believing they were in the right and each labeling those who felt or thought differently as their enemies. I saw people reduced to colors (red for Republican, blue for Democrat). I saw division, polarization, intolerance. Everyone was screaming; no one was listening.

The experience changed me. It opened my eyes to a country not just at war in a foreign land, but with itself.

◆   ◆   ◆

Yet in that same year, there was a young, fresh, vibrant speaker at the Democratic National Convention I had never heard of, speaking of a different kind of politics. He spoke of "E Pluribus Unum" and working together. "There is not a liberal America and a conservative America," he said. "There is the United States of America. There is not a Black America and a White America and Latino America and Asian America—there's the United States of America."

"The pundits," he continued, "the pundits like to slice-and-dice our country into Red States and Blue States; Red States for Republicans, Blue States for Democrats. But I've got news for them, too. We worship an awesome God in the Blue States, and we don't like federal agents poking around in our libraries in the Red States. We coach Little League in the Blue States and yes, we've got some gay friends in the Red States …"

It was a breath of fresh air. Finally, a politician who seemed to understand both the complexity and simplicity of America. A politician with a story that epitomized what was good in our country. A politician who didn't seem phony or jaded or rehearsed, but genuine and real. A politician, finally, who resonated for me.

◆   ◆   ◆

A couple of years later, in 2006, I was changed again when I learned that a close friend of mine I had met while serving a mission for my church in Micronesia had joined the military. Within the year he was sent to Baghdad and killed. He was 21.

The news hurt me deeply. It made me angry. I felt he had been used unnecessarily. He had his whole life ahead of him, with so much good to offer the world. And now he was gone.

Yet clear back in 2002, the year this tragic war was being planned and pitched by the Bush Administration and gaining broad support from Americans and Congress alike, a little known state senator from Illinois had this to say:

> After September 11th, after witnessing the carnage and destruction, the dust and the tears, I supported this Administration's pledge to hunt down and root out those who would slaughter innocents in the name of intolerance, and I would willingly take up arms myself to prevent such a tragedy from happening again …
>
> I'm not opposed to all wars. I'm opposed to dumb wars.… I know that even a successful war against Iraq will require a US occupation of undetermined length, at undetermined cost, with undetermined consequences. I know that an invasion of Iraq without a clear rationale and without strong international support will only fan the flames of the Middle East, and encourage the worst, rather than best, impulses of the Arab world, and strengthen the recruitment arm of al-Qaeda …

> That's what I'm opposed to. A dumb war. A rash war. A war based not on reason but on passion, not on principle but on politics.

Indeed, when others said what was popular or political, or even made a genuine mistake, Barack Obama had the vision and moral courage to see the war for what it was. I appreciated that. I respected that. I knew if he were leading the country my friend would be alive, as would thousands of other American soldiers and Iraqi civilians. That meant something to me.

◆   ◆   ◆

What solidified my support of Barack Obama was reading his book, *The Audacity of Hope.* What struck me the most was its honesty. Like many other young Americans coarsened by a lifetime of empty political rhetoric, I wasn't so naïve as to view Obama as a savior, or the answer to all of America's problems; but I did respect his ability to tell the truth about some of the realities of modern day politics, to genuinely understand and sympathize with both sides of complex issues like abortion, and perhaps most importantly, his tendency to actually listen to his constituents. Obama, I realized, was not raised in bureaucracy, he was not a CEO or governor; he was a community organizer. He was accustomed to working *with* people not above them. He believed that average citizens like me mattered and were the key to transforming America.

This idea of re-invigorating the role of citizenship spoke to my generation.

As I read Obama, I was reminded of what Robert F. Kennedy said over 35 years earlier:

> The world's hope ... is to rely on youth. The cruelties and the obstacles of this swiftly changing planet will not yield to obsolete dogmas and outworn slogans. It cannot be moved by those who cling to a present which is already dying, who prefer the illusion of security to the excitement and danger which comes with even the most peaceful progress. This world demands the qualities of youth: not a time of life but a state of mind, a temper of the will, a quality of imagination, a predominance of courage over timidity, of the appetite for adventure over the life of ease ... it is the young people who must take the lead.

◆   ◆   ◆

So I woke up early on February 10, 2007 and felt chills as I saw a different kind of politician walk up the steps to the majestic Old State Capitol building where Abraham Lincoln once told the country that "a house divided against itself cannot stand." It didn't take MSNBC's Chris Matthews to help me understand I was witnessing history. More than 17,000 people came and braved the freezing weather to be there and listen. As *Newsweek*'s Howard Fineman described it:

> It was more than worth the brief discomfort [of the cold] to witness the scene: the lean figure of Obama, framed by the Greek revival capitol, its worn limestone golden in the morning sun; the young, multi-cultural crowd cheering for him; the echoes of Lincoln and the Heartland; the whistles of the freight trains … America at its best.

◆   ◆   ◆

And so we have this book, a book that is a representation—a symbol and a clarion call—of a movement.

It is about young people feeling empowered, feeling their voices matter, organizing and mobilizing across the country in an unprecedented way. It is about grassroots groups springing up by the thousands online and then translating into massive turnouts in Iowa and New Hampshire, South Carolina and California, Nevada and Texas. It's about over 300,000 young people joining a Facebook group whose goal is to garner "one million strong for Barack." It's about record-setting donations coming primarily from regular people, not special interests. It's about young people working together, using what time and talent and resources they can manage to create events, fundraisers, voter registration drives, blogs, and videos.

As one journalist wrote after witnessing an incredibly successful student-organized rally at George Mason University that drew over 3,500 people:

> What happened at George Mason provided physical evidence that Obama's youth following is more than a bunch of kids who clicked a button…. The mainstream media tends to portray the Obama youth movement as a pack of groupies, fawning over the latest rock star. But these students have shown that they're not interested in being spectators.

Indeed, if that message hasn't been sent yet, it will be felt with force on election day when hundreds of thousand of young voters will be hitting the polls for the first time.

In his announcement speech, Barack Obama described his vision of the movement this way:

> This campaign can't only be about me. It must be about us—it must be about what we can do together. This campaign must be the occasion, the vehicle, of your hopes, and your dreams. It will take your time, your energy, and your advice—to push us forward when we're doing right, and to let us know when we're not. This campaign has to be about reclaiming the meaning of citizenship, restoring our sense of common purpose, and realizing that few obstacles can withstand the power of millions of voices calling for change.

This book is our collective voice, our call for that change. It is a project conceived of, created, and carried out by young Americans. The essays come from all over the country, from Los Angeles to New York, Kansas to Illinois. The prompt was to answer a simple question: Why Obama?

These are our answers—and for these 25 there are doubtless millions of others from Generations X, Y, and Z, who are paying attention, discussing, coordinating, mobilizing—preparing to shock the world in 2008.

1

Dare to Hope

○ ○
Farouk Aregbe is the founder of One Million Strong for Barack, an online group that generated national attention for garnering over 300,000 young people in a matter of weeks. He is a recent alumnus of North Dakota University and currently resides in Washington, D.C.

It's not unprecedented to hear young visionary leaders strike the moral chord of a generation. From Kennedy and King we learned to "ask not what our country could do for us but what we could do for our country," and we subscribed to the dream that we had a say in making our country better.

So when another young gentleman named Barack Obama stepped to the podium in Boston in 2004, we were again reminded that this is the United States of America—the land of liberty, the cradle of freedom in the modern world. In that speech, we witnessed again the merging power of a great mind and a great idea.

As I glance at the field of candidates in the upcoming elections, I am reminded that this nation indeed has many great minds—even in politics. However, too often these minds are restricted by the inability to communicate and work together in a sensible manner. There is no doubt that our policy makers have many plans—plans to escalate war or de-escalate war, plans for life or for choice, plans to define or redefine marriage, plans for more national security or more civil liberties.

Yet in all these plans, there doesn't seem to be much listening. America needs a plan to listen and hear the beckoning call of those crying in Darfur and in Iraq and even in our own backyard here in the United States, in New Orleans. Loud as it may be, this is a call that we cannot hear while we bicker across party lines and pay little attention to the real problems at hand.

We desperately need our leaders to reach across the legislative aisle, leaders that will work together to move the nation forward. I do not believe for a second that Barack Obama has all the answers to every question that we face in America; however, I do believe that he is the one who has the audacity to put aside his pride and get answers from anyone who might have them in order to find meaningful solutions to the problems that we face as a country. That in itself sets him apart.

◆   ◆   ◆

When I created the group One Million Strong for Barack on Facebook on January 16th, 2007, I had no earthly idea that young people all across America were so thirsty for a new kind of leadership. But I soon realized that people young and old, rich and poor, democrat, republican or independent were ready for the kind of reasonable, sensible and responsible politics that will reach across our differences to carry this country forward. That's what Barack Obama seemed to offer people. Within days, people were joining this online group by the thousands, inviting friends, and raising funds.

What was once a simple idea has now exploded into something far greater than myself: over 350,000 people have joined this group and the number continues to grow every day.

This grassroots interest was further stressed by the over 3,500 students that showed up for the "Yes We Can!" rally at George Mason University in Fairfax, Virginia (before Obama had even officially announced). I was invited to speak at the occasion by another grassroots organization, Students for Barack Obama. It was also the first time I had the chance to meet Senator Obama. The most amazing thing about that experience was how *truly genuine* Barack Obama is.

Up until that point, I'd heard many speeches and speakers, seen quite a bit of politics and policies in the 26 years of my life. But in that moment, I was convinced that this was the dawn of a new day in politics. It was an incredible experience. I stood there for 30 minutes, soaked in the words I heard and thought to myself, "What a beautiful future America has in store."

2

My Political Awakening

○ ○

Sarah R. Carter is currently a PhD candidate in Neuroscience at UC-San Francisco, where her research focuses on the molecular mechanisms and intracellular signaling pathways that underlie learning and memory. She was born in Georgia, grew up in Evanston, Illinois, and is the granddaughter of former president Jimmy Carter.

While I was growing up, I was always aware of what was going on politically, but I was never involved. My whole family would tell stories about the magical 1976 campaign with all of its people and places and speeches and rallies. But all of that was before my time. For most of my adult life, I figured that I had missed my chance to participate in politics. I would vote, but that was about it. I had never volunteered for a campaign, never gone to a rally, and never given money to someone running for office.

Until one day in June, 2003, when a convergence of events thrust me into political action.

That year, Barack Obama was beginning his run in a crowded primary for the US Senate in Illinois. In June, when I visited my mom in Evanston, Illinois, I got a chance to meet him. I was on a break from graduate school, sitting around on a Saturday morning, and my mom told me that she and my step-dad were going to a Barack Obama fundraiser and that I should come. They told me who he was on the way to downtown Chicago: he was a state senator; he had spoken out against the Iraq war; he had worked for healthcare for all children; he had worked against the death penalty; he was the first black president of the *Harvard Law Review*; he had been a community organizer on the South side; in short, he just seemed like a great guy.

The fundraiser was a relatively low-key event at a condo belonging to a friend of my mom's—there were only about 50 people there, and I was only a little underdressed in my jeans. I was by far the youngest person there; many of the guests were white suburban ladies older than my mom.

Obama was as great as we hoped he'd be. He was an impressive and convincing speaker. He was very knowledgeable, but very humble; he and his single staffer listened carefully while those older ladies (political veterans themselves) gave advice about how to handle suburban voters and about the pitfalls of previous candidates. He seemed like he was ambitious, but comfortable. He was someone who really believed that politics could do good. He believed that he was someone who had the power, and therefore, the responsibility to take charge. It was obvious to everyone at that fundraiser that he was going places—even if he didn't win that first primary, he would some day be in a position to make some changes.

Recently, I read an old article in *Salon* by Scott Turow. In it, he describes Obama this way: "To be young, black and brilliant has always appeared to me to be one of the more extraordinary burdens in American life. Much is offered; even more is expected. You are like a walking Statue of Liberty, holding up the torch 24 hours a day. Yet Barack Obama, who spent his early years coming to terms with his heritage, is in every sense comfortable in his own skin and committed to a political vision far broader than racial categories."

I thought this paragraph really hit the nail on the head; it described him perfectly. Before I left the fundraiser, my Mom was surprised and pleased that I wrote a check to the Obama campaign for $50. It was my first political contribution.

It was at that fundraiser that another friend of my Mom's asked me if I'd voted in the MoveOn.org primary yet. I had to ask what MoveOn.org was. She told me that I should sign up to get on their email list and to vote for Howard Dean. I had barely heard his name before. Soon after that, I became a big Howard Dean supporter—I hung around at DeanforAmerica.com, reloading the comment board compulsively and, if the campaign was having a big fundraising push, I'd check up on its progress several times a day. I gave money, joined the Dean Corps and told anyone who would listen that Howard Dean was the best candidate.

These days, I am very active in politics and political campaigns. My most significant work for a political campaign was for my dad, Jack Carter, who ran for US Senate in Nevada in 2006. In addition to going door-to-door, phone banking, helping to organize rallies and making sure they ran smoothly, and generally doing whatever needed doing, I was in charge of internet outreach. A large part of that was interacting with the major political blogs Daily Kos and MyDD, posting blog entries that would update people on the status of the campaign and ask them for their time and money. It was through Howard Dean's website that I discovered political blogs. It was my experience with the blogosphere that made me valuable to my Dad's campaign.

That Obama fundraiser really set into motion a series of events that changed my life forever. It was Barack Obama himself that made me feel that a single person could make a difference and that I had a responsibility to participate in the political process.

When Obama's presidential campaign launched, I watched his announcement speech on the website and signed up on my.BarackObama.com as soon as it was available. I had been following his career; I was happy when he easily won his Senate race, and exhilarated when he gave his now-famous speech at the National Democratic Convention in 2004. Most recently, on Saturday, March 17, 2007 I volunteered to help with the big Obama rally held in Oakland, California. Obama gave an excellent speech, and the 10,000-plus people who came left very excited. As a volunteer, I had to show up early and stay a little bit late. I was there for a total of almost six hours, and I was happy to be a part of it.

My days of political apathy are now squarely behind me. I am now not only aware, but determined to be involved in making our country better. And I can trace my political awakening to that small meeting in Illinois when I first met Barack Obama.

3

Finding Hope in an Age of Skepticism

○ ○
Stephen McIntyre grew up in Claremont, California. He recently graduated magna cum laude from Brigham Young University with a Bachelor of Arts in Chinese, and is currently pursuing a Juris Doctor and a Master of Arts in East Asian Studies at Duke University. He has been married for two years. His wife, Nicole, teaches elementary school.

Mine is a skeptical generation, and perhaps rightfully so. The political era in which we have come of age has been neither glorious nor flattering. Between constant headlines of fraud, scandal, and corruption, raging ideological battles, incessant mud-slinging, and widespread disappointment with the current administration, it has become apparent to thousands of young Americans from all walks of life that something is not right in Washington. We have been conditioned to look at our elected officials with an untrusting eye, because all too often those in whom the electorate has placed its trust have left promises unfulfilled and expectations unmet. There is a growing consensus, not just on college campuses but among Americans at large, that it is time for a change in American politics.

Fortunately, our Founding Fathers endowed the citizenry of the United States of America with the means to "provide new Guards for their future security." Americans voiced their dissatisfaction last November by casting their ballots, dramatically altering our legislative bodies. My generation was particularly vocal; the proportion of young voters that participated in the 2006 congressional election was the highest in at least twenty years. We sense the urgency of making certain that peace, prosperity, opportunity, and justice are still the defining virtues of the America that we and future generations will inherit. While I still have hope for the prospects of the congress we elected, the problems that have plagued politics in recent years cannot be attributed to a particular party or politician; both Democrats and Republicans have been guilty of the same faults. Some of the players may have changed, but I fear that we are essentially playing the same game. What we need is a new brand of politics, one governed by integrity, sincerity, cooperation, and pragmatism. We need a government that is not only attentive to the needs of its people but also capable of implementing productive and efficient policy in their service, despite differences in opinion, ideology, and party affiliation. We need a president like Barack Obama to help make this type of government a reality.

Although I initially reacted to this junior senator's presidential prospects with cynicism, his political philosophy caught my attention. It wasn't his views on the Iraq war, health care, or the environment that most impressed me—although, his progressive approach to these and other current issues is one of his strengths—but rather, his vision of a politics in which "distortion, name-calling, and sound-bite solutions to complicated problems" are replaced by openness, accountability, and integrity. Barack Obama has fought to raise the standards to which public servants are held, most recently helping to pass the Legislative Transparency and Accountability Act of 2007, which has been hailed as "the strongest ethics legislation to emerge from Congress yet." He insists upon grounding government in "[g]enuine bipartisanship," in which there is "an honest process of give-and-take" and "the quality of the compromise is measured by how well it serves some agreed-upon goal." Although devoted to Democratic Party values, Obama dares to traverse the no-man's land of moderation and compromise that exists between party lines in the interest of pragmatism and problem-solving. In both the Illinois Senate and the U.S. Senate, Barack Obama has a history of working with Republicans in passing needed legislation. As leader of this nation, President Obama will continue to redefine American politics, placing action before ideology, seeking cooperation rather than alienation, and restoring the trust between government and citizen. Obama's approach to politics has allowed me to again believe in the possibility that "there are better days ahead." I am confident that as Barack Obama continues to help us reform American politics, "people will work hard, ... the entire economy will grow[,] everyone will benefit and more resources will be available for all, not just select groups."

I believe that one of Barack Obama's greatest strengths lies in his conviction that "the greatness of our nation ... is based on [the] very simple premise ...

[']that all men are created equal … [and] are endowed by their Creator with certain unalienable rights.'" While successive tax cuts have been awarded to the wealthy and the number of Americans living in poverty has grown by over five million under the Bush administration, Barack Obama seeks to ensure that each citizen is equally privileged with the opportunity to succeed and participate in the shaping of our national destiny. He reminds us that "we have a stake in one another, and … what binds us together is greater than what drives us apart." In other words, it is in my interest to see that my fellow citizens receive an education, have access to affordable health care, and work at a job that allows them to support a family. His refreshing call for "an America that's about not just each of us, but all of us" has reminded me of the obligation I have to other Americans, especially those who are less fortunate than me. Having worked as a community organizer in poor Chicago neighborhoods, Barack Obama draws from a wealth of personal experience in recognizing and addressing the needs of our lower and middle classes. He challenges the government and the American people to invest in public education, make college affordable, modernize our health care system, use energy resources responsibly, and devise new strategies to protect our nation from terror. Because our collective success is dependent upon the successes of individual Americans, we need a president that is devoted to the realization of these goals. In short, the United States of America needs Barack Obama.

Barack Obama's hopes for America are indeed, as he puts it, "audacious." In this cynical age, skeptics like me may be tempted to accuse him of being unrealistic, perhaps even naïve. The problems facing America are daunting, yes, but they are by no means unconquerable. In announcing his candidacy for President of the United States, Senator Obama declared that "few obstacles can withstand the power of millions of voices calling for change." As Americans, it is our privilege and duty to correct our nation's course and secure a brighter future. I am proud to join with Barack Obama in putting behind us an age marked by pettiness, division, and inequality, and once again "take up the unfinished business of perfecting our union, and building a better America."

4

My Reflection

○ ○

Estevan Carlos Benson works in new media, music, and mixed media as an MFA student in Design/Media Arts at UCLA. His work is featured on his personal website at www.estevancarlos.com. Once he almost drowned in Walden Pond. He says it wasn't fun. His friend said, "How transcendental."

Over the years I've developed the strange habit of avoiding mirrors and looking at my reflection. I avert my eyes when walking by windows across buildings and an unsettling feeling eats away at me.

As a young child, I had a vague sense of the political and cultural atmosphere and how the two collided for me as a kid from a middle-class Mexican family in Texas. I remember a middle school teacher voicing her disapproval of the welfare system while I held a peculiar silence recalling the very brief moment in time when my mother and I received such assistance. At that age I couldn't follow any nuance to the teacher's argument. As a thirteen-year-old boy, I took her remarks as a blanket judgment upon those involved in the system.

Years later on a cold night in Boston, the issue of affirmative action came up with some of my classmates at a coffee shop just outside campus. They expressed their disagreement of the policy as I respectfully listened. College admission should be based solely on grades, they said. We should have the best.

I revealed that I came to this university via an affirmative action program and with a scholarship through the African-American Institute. This wasn't necessarily an argument against them and their views. They were my friends, and I never felt they disapproved of me. Yet their comments affected me.

Even at 21 years of age, I could not offer any cogent defense for my political views. More importantly, I had not yet realized that I didn't need to defend myself. Even in the African-American program, counselors would frequently encourage their students not to hold questionable and insecure feelings about these issues. And I thought I was the only one.

My home life was full of cultural diversity. I am multiracial: Black and Mexican (and Irish and Portuguese if we're counting). My mother would often quietly hide her spiritual and religious views from her peers due to a fear of offending those in our very Catholic and military-centered city.

These worlds of traditional, conservative values mixing with issues of race and religion have at times negated one another. They've created a strange place in between where I have stood for some time. As such, I've lived a somewhat apathetic life—apathetic in my views towards people, race, religion, politics—a life designed as a sort of safety net where I could not find myself arriving at too many conclusions. I've lived an impersonal life for some time ... but they tell me politics is personal.

I ask myself about my hesitations to take politics to heart and try to observe with a keen eye my motivations. As I have become more and more familiar with the Illinois senator, Barack Obama, I find myself returning to that same strange place in between. I wonder if portions of my trust in this man are implicitly connected to our shared multiracial experiences, or what I deem as shared. I question my intentions as I find myself shocked but admiring of a man who looks almost like me accomplishing what he has.

I am no longer the aching, young, eight-year-old boy seeking a father figure. I am now a man—a man experienced in this post-modern, existential world. I have my faults. I can make emotionally-uninformed decisions that are at times objective, fair, and right, at other times, I can be foolish and wrong. Like others, I debate my heart against my mind. In this gray area, those who wish to fault Obama find their supposed justifications. Am I becoming that bleeding heart they shout against? If so, does it truly matter?

Barack Obama is a politician and so I coyly admit that I don't want to approve of him. But his lack of political calculation is something I hold as an attribute, one that is difficult to maintain in his line of work. Right now, as we speak, the debate seems to be whether Obama is black enough. Whether he is black? What does it even mean to be black? How black is black enough? It's a challenging and complex discussion, but strangely it outshines the real debate of his policies. It glazes over the real issues of our society's slow, ignorant, and naïve understanding of race, including my own.

Among my strewn thoughts on America, race, and the pulls of my heart and resolute desire of mind, I've come to the conclusion that Barack Obama is uniquely American. Absurdly American. A phenomenon that is almost exclusive to our American experience. His life story touches so many, not only for its scope but because it represents the lesser-recognized, social facets of our nation. It represents that we not only offer education and opportunity but that we as a nation offer a platform for a new culture.

Obama is almost an invention of America just as so many of us are.

Whatever my hesitations, I have to arrive at some conclusions. Despite the conflicts of my mind, heart, history, heritage and beliefs, I will arrive at some conclusions.

I do support Barack Obama.

This presidential run is about what I learned in the most earnest of cities: San Antonio, Texas. It is about the values I picked up from the laborers and blue collar workers, from my mother who worked day and night to support us. This is about my experiences in Boston and Cambridge, Massachusetts: the anti-war rallies, open discussions of gender and sexual orientation, discussions of race and religion. This presidential run is about our ability to be challenged by our taboos, our current political climate, and the wonderful unison of our hearts and minds, individually and as a nation.

Am I misinformed? Am I confused? This time around, I can confidently say "No." I make no apologies. My trust in Obama is not narrow, just as my life experience is not either.

I realize now my fear of my reflection was a fear of my face, my ideas, and what I represent. It's been a fear of not knowing if I am embraced by this nation, embraced by a community, or anything else. They are personal issues which I know well enough not to let solely influence my decision on Barack Obama. My open support for Obama is my means of dissolving those fears.

It is fool-hearted to support a man because he looks like you. It is great to support a man because he represents you and so many others of this nation.

5

Joining the Conversation

○ ○
Akin Salawu is an alumnus of both Stanford and Columbia University. He was awarded the Sherifa Omada Edoga Prize for his role in founding and running a culturally diverse theatre group. Akin interned at Kopelson Entertainment, Donner/Shuler-Donner, and Dreamworks SKG before working on the New Orleans season of the MTV reality show *The Real World*. Akin currently lives in New Jersey and has more or less devoted his personal website www.atthatdrop.com and filmmaking skills to the grassroots effort to support Senator Obama's presidential campaign.

The first time I voted, I voted for the guy my high school government teacher told us to vote for. She had taken the time to register her students to vote so following her suggestion seemed like the right thing to do. I hadn't taken my Government class as seriously as I took AP Calculus so it follows that I did not take my voting privilege particularly seriously.

Fall quarter freshman year at Stanford the campus's common consciousness was heavily skewed towards the candidate I had been introduced to in high school so I never had to defend my candidate. Contrary to the popular argument that a teacher should not share her political beliefs with her students, my high school government teacher should be commended for believing that her voting-aged students mattered enough to warrant convincing.

With the exception of the two people who have thrown down the gauntlet at the sight of my "Barack Obama President 2008" button, my high school government teacher is, to date, the only person to ever make a significant attempt to influence my vote. Given the historically low voter turnout amongst Black Americans, others must have figured I probably would not be showing up at the polls so making a play for my vote would prove a futile effort.

Fast forward four years: Election Day finds me on a studio lot doing extra work. The production company made special arrangements to allow everyone working on the film to go vote. I was often asked which candidate I thought was going to win the Black Vote. Fortunately, I knew very little about the candidate I was not voting for so I answered the question by riffing on the concept of a Black Vote.

Although Bluetooth headsets resemble the headgear worn by the Borg on Star Trek, Black Americans are not automaton drones networked to a hive mind Borg Queen. There are no monthly "Black in America" meetings where we get together to hash out what "we" think. I've yet to come across a newsletter reviewing the Black American Political Agenda, although I'm certain someone somewhere is distributing such a document. This is part of why I love America. Some well-meaning fellow in St. Louis can kick back atop a ferry boat at Laclede's Landing with a cold lemonade in his hand and decide to write and distribute his political agenda and no one will stop him. He'll face his fair share of obstacles, but for the most part, systems are in place to facilitate his crusade.

Each and every Black American citizen has just as much freedom to determine his or her vote as any other American. While there may be a greater level of support for one candidate than another, there is no formula for decoding who most Black Americans will vote for just as there is no formula for decoding what brand of fabric softener most Black Americans will purchase. Reverends may point their congregants in one direction. The local community activist groups may nudge their members in the opposite direction. Some voters go with the candidate who their Wall Street co-workers have all agreed to get behind. Some voters go with the candidate who reminds them of that guy who cleared away the tree that crashed into the Township Library after it was struck by lightning. And if he perseveres, some voters will even support that fellow up on the ferry boat at Laclede's Landing because his kids are at his side faithfully selling lemonade for the cost of a smile.

Just before the following presidential election, I moved from California to New Jersey and couldn't be bothered with absentee voting so I took myself out of the process without a second thought. I figured the party I had voted for twice would win the election without my vote. Of course, the first time I neglected to vote, my party lost. I hadn't officially perceived them as my party, but the juxtaposition of a loss the first time I didn't step up to the polls fostered a sense of allegiance. Both California and New Jersey went to my party so my vote would not have changed the election's outcome. Still, the lesson echoes: I did not participate in the political conversation so the conversation went on without me and ultimately did not go my way.

I was in graduate film school at Columbia University for the next presidential election. Election Day was my birthday, November 2. A friend was registering people to vote so he helped me with my change of address registration. This election was sure to be as controversial as the last so I knew I had to be on point to participate in the conversation. I never got my voter registration confirmation card so I called around to find out what had happened. I was informed that whoever typed my information into the system misspelled my name so I was not going to be able to vote. I shrugged at the gauntlet now at my feet. I was mulling over how to pick the gauntlet up when justice smiled on me and I booked a freelance job that required me to work out of the state on Election Day. I proudly voted absentee. I participated in the conversation. Yet, after all that, my party lost. I decided I was done with the conversation. In any flawed conversation, either the participants are flawed or the process is flawed. I had participated freely and fairly so it must have been the process. Clearly my voice was insignificant, the mountain of books I still needed to read was almost as tall as Shaquille O'Neal, and HBO's original programming was getting better and better, so why should I spend anymore time and energy in the political conversation?

Finally, several months ago I stumbled upon a streamed video clip of Senator Obama speaking at a banquet on the Harvard Law School website. I had previously read *The Audacity of Hope* as a Utopian Fantasy written by a writer who adopted an optimistic voice to sell his book. After seeing his speech given at Harvard, I realized this was a man who genuinely still believes. In spite of his time in D.C., Senator Barack Obama still believes in the potential of progress towards a Utopian American Reality. I downloaded *The Audacity of Hope* and now listen to it on my iPod when I'm exercising or driving long distances.

The sense that maybe I can participate in the conversation in an effective manner has inspired a number of changes. I attend panels, discussions, and grassroots "support Senator Obama" meetings. I've more or less devoted my personal website to the grassroots effort and other socially conscious causes. I've been immersed into a community of other people who are inspired by the possibility, the possibility that we have found a man willing to think about solutions from the citizen's perspective. Suddenly I'm excited about politics. Suddenly people all around me are excited about politics. In a Central Jersey bar a few twenty-somethings asked about my button and I told them Senator Obama was against the war from the start. They got all riled up about the new generation of Vets. Eyes blazed as these Gen X & Gen Y guys spoke fondly of childhood friends who are still overseas. The hunger for hope of safe returns was infectious and each story led to someone else chiming in about the kid he used to play kickball with down the street. Then I asked who was registered to vote and the wind fell out of most of the sails in the place; however, the silver lining glowed vibrantly. I saw that I could focus my efforts towards turning the apathy, disappointment, and disdain so many of us have struggled with into an active need to get to the polls and participate in the conversation. Thanks to Senator Barack Obama, we are going to see more Black Americans, more Gen-Xers, and more Gen-Yers participating in the conversation. Thanks to Senator Obama my voice is already being heard.

6

Just a poor kid from Ohio

○ ○
Aaron Hatfield is currently a senior at Van Wert High School in
Ohio. He is a member of the Van Wert YMCA and enjoys play-
ing basketball, music and hanging out with friends.

I am 18 years old and from Ohio. I have never been involved in politics or even
cared much about it. Sure, I have seen plenty of politicians talking on TV, but
until Barack Obama I never actually heard any of them. Their message was not
for me. I figured none of those Washington big shots cared about a poor kid in
Van Wert, Ohio.

Then I heard the speech Barack gave in Illinois and you know what? I felt like
he was talking to me, that he cared about my problems. I stopped dead in my
tracks and sat down and listened and I thought, "Hey, this guy Obama, he ain't
like those other guys. He wants to help all people, not just the rich and famous."

Ever since I was a little kid I have heard my folks talking about JFK and RFK
and how they brought hope to America. They say they are feeling that hope again
for the first time in a long time. I know that Barack Obama speaks for me; in fact,
I think he speaks for us all.

He is the voice of hope, the voice of reason, and the voice of the future.

I feel like I even have a voice now. I think a president needs to be more then
just a politician, he needs to also be an inspiration—not just to Americans but to
the world. If ever the world needed a man like Barack it's now!

I plan to get registered and to vote for the first time in 2008 for the next President of the United States, Mr. Barack Obama, the voice of hope.

7

A Vision for a Better World

o o o o o o o o o o o o o o o o o o o o o o o o o o o o o o o o

Dean Burrier will be a senior at Western Reserve Academy in
the fall of 2007. He plays three varsity sports: basketball, track
and cross country. He plans to major in History in college.

"Let the word go forth from this time and place," John F. Kennedy famously pro-
claimed at his presidential inauguration. "To friend and foe alike, that the torch
has been passed to a new generation of Americans—born in this century, tempered by war, disciplined by a hard and bitter peace, proud of our ancient
heritage …"

I was not there that day, but I can imagine how awe-inspiring it must have
been to hear his words. I memorized a portion of that famous inaugural address
when I was in fifth grade. Back then, I couldn't fully grasp the importance of the
words, or comprehend their power. With his words and more importantly his
actions, Kennedy captured the imaginations of the American people and lifted
America out of a slump.

Growing up, I have without a doubt been tempered by war. I attended a small
Christian school from kindergarten through sixth grade. September 11th started
as any normal day did at Chapel Hill Christian School. The principal's voice
beamed over the PA system in our classroom. She went through some routine
announcements and then led us in reciting the Pledge of Allegiance. Every day
since kindergarten had started like this.

Later that same morning, my teacher shared the terrible news of what had
happened. I didn't even know what the World Trade Center was, but I still cried.
A girl sitting next to me asked if I had family or friends in New York. I didn't,
but I cried because I knew something horrible had happened to our country. At
home, I read the newspaper articles and listened intently to Peter Jennings' news

segments all week long. At this time, out of fear, I became politically conscious. The president's words were no remedy for me.

Another event shaped my political consciousness to a greater extent. My parents decided I was going to attend a small prep school for high school. The school's diversity forced me to see the rest of the world as I had never before seen it. I learned to care about the countries my friends and classmates came from. In class, we studied world history in a way that brought it to life. During my second year, the school supported me by affording me a grant to study abroad. In the summer of 2006, I spent the summer in Spain with my brother. It was my first trip to a foreign country and my first time in a city the size of Madrid. I lived with a host-family and attended classes at the University of Madrid. I met people from Germany, Italy, Denmark and many other countries. All the adventures and discoveries transformed me and opened my mind to the world outside of America.

I returned with a new perspective on this world and a great thing happened: I met Chinedu. He had recently come to the United States from Nigeria, where he was raised in an Igbo tribe. Africa always grabs my attention. It's a land so full of culture and history and beauty, but plagued by misconceptions, political struggle and disease. I had read about Chinedu's Igbo people in Chinua Achebe's *Things Fall Apart* and the book only intensified my desire to learn about Africa. Chinedu very quickly became a close friend.

Then the genocide in Darfur, Sudan came to my attention. It was hard to find out the truth of the situation because the newspapers buried the story in the back of the paper. One obvious fact was that America was failing to act or stop the genocide, just like in the 1990s with Rwanda. It angered me that we were allowing a horrifying moment in history to repeat itself.

Then I heard about a senator from Illinois, Barack Obama. He was in Africa, a region that so many of America's politicians forget about, speaking to the people in the streets. His words were soft, yet powerful, and they did not induce fear, but instead hope and optimism. He spoke of a vision for a better world, not just a better America.

From then on I couldn't get enough of Barack Obama. More important than his eloquent words were his more powerful actions. Senator Obama led a march in Washington, D.C calling for U.S. intervention in Darfur. In Congress, Senator Obama has been a powerful voice in so many of Congress' accomplishments. He reminds me of so many of the great leaders that America has had in the past: he is dedicated to the task of serving the American people and follows through with his promises.

Our nation finds itself at a crossroads. So many issues are tearing our country apart, whether it's the war in Iraq, abortion or gay marriage. We, as a people, need a leader who truly represents us and can unite us despite these differences. I believe that Barack Obama can be that leader, a leader who speaks for our generation and unites us for the good of our country and, more importantly, for the good of the world.

As Obama put it on the day of his announcement in Springfield, Illinois: "Each and every time a new generation has risen up and done what needs to be done. Today we are called once more—and it is time for our generation to answer that call."

8

A Nobody's Opinion

o o o o o o o o o o o o o o o o o o o o o o o o o o o o o o o

Billie Zahir is a single mother pursuing a history education degree at Macon State College in Georgia. She has a 14 year old daughter and hopes to soon be a high school history teacher.

I am a nobody.

I grew up in a middle class, middle of the road home and my parents divorced when I was young. I did not like school so I dropped out early and got my GED. I had a child out of wedlock at a time when I should have been going to college. I worked at a job that I hated just to make ends meet.

I have never owned my own home. I have had to make the choice of either buying medication or buying food for my family. I had to move back in with my mother because she had a brain tumor and it was affecting her sight and no doctor would help her because she does not have insurance. I never had time to do those extra things that you dream of doing with your children … like taking a vacation.

I have turned to relationships to lighten the load that I feel. I have found out I suffer from Manic-Depression but was told that the funds were not there to help pay for the treatment that I need. I see the rich getting richer and me and people like me not going anywhere. I went back to school to be the person I wanted to be but still felt I was a nobody.

My problem was I did not know what path to take to become somebody. Somebody is someone whose voice is heard. Somebody is a person who, despite the mistakes that they have made, is looked upon as a person who holds some value. Somebody is a person who is ill and can count on medical care even when they cannot afford it at that moment. Somebody is a person who is empowered to be the best that they can be by the society around them.

In my search to find out how to be a somebody, I found the world is full of a lot of "nobodies" like myself. I see people who are broken and cynical about the state of the nation. I see people who feel like victims. I see people who see the issues in the world and feel like they are powerless. I see people who feel the American dream is either dead or out of reach.

But I found a path to becoming a somebody when I discovered Barack Obama. I found a somebody who believed I was not a nobody. I found a somebody who is not offering a handout that would only serve to demoralize me more but a hand up to realize my full potential as a somebody. I found somebody who realizes that only by making all the people in the nation a somebody will we be able to see the American dream become a reality for everyone, not just the elite few. I found a somebody who offers me hope and a chance to be part of something greater than myself.

I am proud to say that now, due to Barack Obama, I am a former nobody who has realized they are somebody. And my greatest hope is that he will have a chance as president to help all those other somebodies like me that have been treated like "nobodies."

9

More than a Game

○ ○

Charley Johnson is a recent graduate of the University of Washington. He interned for the Woodrow Wilson Center, the German Marshall Fund, the Center for Strategic and International Studies, the U.S. Senate, and worked for Teach For America. He currently lives and works in Washington D.C.

Here's the thing: politics should be an instrument of good and a lever of opportunity. Politics should be more than good intentions and high rhetoric. It should help people. It should solve problems. And it should ignite our imagination about what's possible if we work together. But politics have, well, fallen short. Let's face it. Politics have fallen so far short that its promises are seen far more often in diction than in deeds.

Politics, nowadays, more accurately resemble a game. And last summer when I interned for the United States Senate, I had court side seats. I learned the rules of the game quite quickly: team uniforms are mandatory and must be worn at all times—red or blue only, please; stay on your side of the court—do not even think of switching teams, not even for one play; and nothing is out of bounds—name calling and trash talking, in fact, earn bonus points. I have to admit, at first I enjoyed watching the red team and the blue team compete for political points. It made for great entertainment. But the game quickly lost its appeal, and I couldn't help but hope that one day we would all play for the same team.

I am not naïve. I know that stark partisanship and uncompromising ideologies have left in their wake a great political divide. I realize that empty promises and false pretenses have left the American people cynical. Politics are dirty and evil. I get it.

But hear me out. I am not speaking about the kind of change we see every four or eight years. I know that new packaging of old ideas is not enough. I am speaking of the kind of change that comes along once in a generation, the kind of change that transforms our politics. I know it's hard to imagine at this stage in the game. But just think: What if the next President of the United States followed moral precepts but did not claim a monopoly on morality? What if he actually matched bipartisan rhetoric with bipartisan action? And what if he had both the experience and judgment to restore our image abroad and keep America safe? We don't have to imagine in vain. Barack Obama could be this kind of president.

Barack Obama has shown that he follows moral precepts but does not claim a monopoly on morality. His political views are not rooted in a rigid ideology. He instead confronts challenges with clinical thought. Obama projects politics that are principled and practical. He finds common ground between facts and values. In *The Audacity of Hope*, Obama reminds us that "values are faithfully applied to the facts before us, while ideology overrides whatever facts call theory into question." But he also knows that the challenges we face today are too great to disagree on without looking from another's perspective. In fact, empathy, which Senator Obama learned from his mother at a young age, animates his politics. If Barack misbehaved, she would look him in the eye and ask, "How do you think that would make you feel?" If only our politics followed this code. Senator Obama explains that

> I am obligated to try to see the world through George Bush's eyes, no matter how much I may disagree with him. That's what empathy does—it calls us all to task, the conservative and the liberal, the powerful and the powerless, the oppressed and the oppressor. We are all shaken out of our complacency. We are all forced beyond our limited vision. No one is exempt from the call to find common ground.

But empathy by itself is not enough. The right values and the right rhetoric will not transform our politics. Americans want action. Americans wants substance.

Obama matches bipartisan rhetoric with bipartisan action. In his highly touted speeches, Obama reminds us that we are all interconnected. He reminds us that we are not all that different. That we share similar values and have similar hopes. He speaks of bipartisanship and what we can do together. This is not empty rhetoric. In a divisive political climate, Senator Obama has reached across the aisle to tackle big problems with practical solutions. He passed legislation with Senator Richard Lugar (R-IN) to prevent the further proliferation of weapons of mass destruction. He worked with Senator Sam Brownback (R-KS) to give a voice to the voiceless Sudanese ravaged by genocide in Darfur. Senator Obama raised CAFÉ fuel economy standards, lifted the veil on earmark and contract spending, spurred the production of alternative diesels, expanded manufacturing for flexible fuel vehicles, provided a tax credit for gas stations that install ethanol refueling pumps, passed legislation to help make college more affordable, expanded learning opportunities for children and helped ensure that our veterans are cared for and housed. He did all of these things hand in hand with Republicans. In a polarized Washington, Senator Obama made America more safe, more energy independent, and made government more transparent and accountable to the American public.

To be sure, Senator Obama's rhetoric has inspired millions of Americans imagination for a new generation of politics. In his announcement for president in Springfield, Illinois, for example, he acknowledged,

> We all made this journey for a reason. It's humbling, but in my heart I know you didn't come here just for me, you came here because you believe in what this country can be. In the face of war, you believe there can be peace. In the face of despair, you believe there can be hope. In the face of a politics that's shut you out, that's told you to settle, that's divided us for too long, you believe we can be one people, reaching for what's possible, building that more perfect union.

I have heard these words before—more than once. We all have. But before Obama, the words did not seem believable. They did not seem authentic. But when I listened to Obama speak, the hair on my arm stood on end. The smile on my face could not be wiped away. For the first time in a long time these words were supported with substance. Obama's words were affirmed by a detailed record that demonstrates exactly what can be accomplished if bipartisan rhetoric is met with bipartisan action.

Obama has the experience and judgment to restore our image abroad and keep America safe. Experience and judgment are not mutually exclusive. Years and years of experience without good judgment only show a candidate's age. Before boots hit the ground, Obama said of the plan to go to war with Iraq, "I don't oppose all wars. And I know that in this crowd today, there is no shortage of patriots, or of patriotism. What I am opposed to is a dumb war. What I am opposed to is a rash war." He went on to argue that the invasion would lead to an occupation of "undetermined length, at undetermined costs, with undetermined consequences." Unfortunately, Senator Obama's judgment proved spot on.

Since the war began, Senator Obama has not looked back. He has not been stuck in the mud, content with criticism. He has led. He has focused on what can be done to end the war responsibly. In November 2005, Senator Obama put forth a plan to reduce the number of U.S. troops, set a time frame for phased withdrawal, impel the Iraqi government to form a political solution, improve reconstruction efforts and restore basic services in Iraq, and engage neighboring states diplomatically. This was later echoed by the bipartisan Iraq Study Group led by James Baker and Lee Hamilton. On the issue of Iraq, Senator Obama has been a bright light amongst a bunch of dead bulbs. His judgment proved prophetic. His criticisms have been consistent but constructive. His plan for our future involvement has been clear.

Senator Obama gives me reason to believe that politics can be an instrument of good and a lever of opportunity. That it can be more than good intentions and high rhetoric. That it can help people and solve problems. Senator Obama gives me reason to believe that politics can be more than a game. Just imagine, what if we were all on the same team and pursued victory together? What if "bipartisanship" was more than rhetoric? What if the next President of the United States was Barack Obama? These questions do not have to be questions. They can be reality.

10

Back to the Beginning

° °
Kristine Deku just moved back to Newport Beach, California, where she was born and raised. She currently works as a Patient Advocate at the Share Our Selves free clinic in Costa Mesa. She has spent the past eight years living in North Carolina, first earning her B.A. at Davidson College and then working in Durham, but decided to move closer to family and home. Next year she hopes to return to school and study pediatric nursing. Her ultimate goals are to work in pediatric oncology and to teach future generations of nursing students.

My family tree teems with strong, politically engaged, and yes, liberal, women. We often can be heard breaking the traditional mealtime taboos against discussing politics and religion, and the conversation is more than likely dominated by female voices. More than once my sister or I have been encouraged to run for office in the future. But every time the subject is broached, I have recoiled in horror and pronounced that despite my passion for justice and my interest in the issues, the price to pay for a life in American politics is too high.

And I am not alone. My peer group of twenty-something voters is statistically the least active and most disenchanted with politics. For many of us, the only president we have known as adults is George W. Bush. We are tired of seeing our nation misled by an administration that seems to have no interest in how most of us are living our lives. Frustrated with the state of politics in this nation, we have distanced ourselves from the games and accepted the inevitable reality that a government designed by and for the people today no longer belongs to us.

But the tide, it seems, is beginning to turn. The first indication to me that change was in the wind occurred during the 2004 Democratic Presidential Convention. I had heard that a Senate candidate from Illinois named Barack Obama would be delivering the keynote address. Word was that his father was from Kenya, a fact which intrigued me because my husband is from Ghana, also on the great continent of Africa. So I tuned in to see this man with whom the news media and convention-goers seemed to have already established a love affair.

Moments later, I figured out why. Here stood a man who was telling me and millions of other Americans that it didn't have to be this way. The America he envisioned was not color-coded along red and blue lines. By the end of the night it was clear that a new kind of politician had emerged.

It would be an understatement to say that this little-known state senator has made some waves since 2004. First he earned an improbable U.S. Senate victory and now, only three years later, Barack Obama is running for President of the United States. He has managed to mobilize hundreds of thousands of young adults as volunteers and raised millions of dollars in tiny increments of $25 or $50 or even $10. Back in 2004, I dreamed that this might happen but never imagined that it would be possible in our current political climate.

Never in my adult life has so much attention been paid to a candidate this early in the race by this many young people. And yet, the media has chalked it up to his so-called "rock star" appeal. We have been reduced to groupies, rather than genuine supporters with substantive reasons for backing Obama. Charm and charisma he may have, but no one can tell us that our support for the next President of the United States is that superficial. We listen to Barack Obama and we support his campaign because he respects us and our intelligence.

Many times I have heard that this "Obama-mania" is akin to the 1960s fervor over John F. Kennedy. My generation was not around to witness JFK's momentous rise to the top, but we all know that once again we are witnessing history in the making. Obama has inspired millions because he understands exactly what this is all supposed to be about. What sets him apart from every other candidate, Democrat or Republican, is that his "different kind of politics" is about us, the American people.

Obama's successes as an attorney and constitutional law professor, and as the first African-American president of the *Harvard Law Review*, demonstrate to us his unquenchable thirst for knowledge and a tireless work ethic. His loving relationship with his family and commitment to their well-being reassures us that he understands how important it is to be surrounded by people whom we love and who love us. His roots as a community organizer encourage us that his political ambitions in Washington are led by a concern not for personal glory but for the people. We believe in Barack Obama because he has a vision for America that invites us all to participate. When he appeared at a rally at George Mason University in February, he told us, "At each and every junction of our history, somebody's been audacious enough to say we can do something different; and more often than not it's been young people who've done it."

As I have listened to President Bush insist that he is "The Decider," I have an image of a pouting toddler mired in a battle of wills. With Bush and others like him, it seems politics has become about power, about making decisions just because you can. In word and deed, the current Administration is telling us that whatever opinions the American people have are irrelevant. We hear in the president's speeches that he'll listen to anyone so long as they agree with him. They have lost sight of the whole point of American government.

Obama's vision reflects a shift away from power plays and fear-mongering toward genuine concern for our everyday well-being. Success for most of us is not defined by how well the stock market did last quarter. Our concerns have more to do with the basic pillars of everyday life: education, employment, health and well-being, and opportunity.

This country is not on a level playing field. The story of the self-made man is memorable precisely because it is unusual. Those who struggle and those who "have not" are left to fend for themselves, told condescendingly that if they just work harder they too can live the American Dream. Senator Obama understands that his story, as inspiring as it is, has not come easily. At the George Mason rally he called on us to recognize that the opportunities we have had do not come to everyone, telling us that there are "young people out there just as talented, just as deserving as you that never get a shot." With Barack Obama in the White House, I believe that will change.

And let us not forget Obama's courageous opposition to the war in Iraq even before we invaded, when President Bush's approval ratings were sky high and speaking out against it was a political liability. Many other 2008 presidential candidates supported or voted to authorize the war back in 2003 and are now backpedaling furiously to explain why they have changed their tunes. Senator Obama was vocally opposed from the beginning.

While the arguments against supporting Obama may be understandable at first glance, a closer look reveals their flaws. Take the "lack of experience" reasoning. In my book, that is not a liability but a strength in today's political climate. Obama has been preparing for this moment since he was my age, during his days as a community organizer. He has elected against learning the steps to the twisted tango that is Washington politics. He has not been poisoned by partisanship; he knows that accomplishing anything for the American people takes hard work and cooperation. And this has been recognized not only by his own party members, but by scores of Republicans. His service on a number of powerful committees—Senate Foreign Relations, Homeland Security, Veterans' Affairs, and Health, Education, Labor and Pensions—shows that he is serious about the issues that affect America and that he has earned the respect of the Senate leadership to justify these appointments. Lack of long-term experience in Washington is not a weakness if you know how to get answers to your questions and have the good judgment to surround yourself with people who know those answers. No president is the authority on everything; this is where the Cabinet, Joint Chiefs of Staff and White House advisors come in, and why the power of the president is held in check by two equally important branches of government.

Another anti-Obama argument is that "liberals" just support Obama because he is Black and we want to show off how progressive we are. If it were merely a matter of guilt or challenging the status quo, then I, a self-professed feminist, should also be supporting Hillary Clinton, which I do not. The most powerful office in the world is not the place to make a social statement for the sake of the statement itself. No person garners the support that Obama has because of an epidemic of liberal guilt. Millions of people are backing him because he gives us hope for the future. His ethnicity and heritage have made him all the more appealing because we see in him a reflection of the way the world has changed in our lifetime. His own parents crossed cultures and broke American anti-miscegenation laws to be together. He was educated for four years in Indonesia, and lived in Hawaii, an extremely diverse state. For many years of his life, he was raised by a single mother. Obama's story resonates with all of us whose own backgrounds are a little "out of the box." He represents a new reality, where the lines that separate us can begin to blur and we can come together.

Finally, there is the rhetoric that "America is not ready for a Black president." I am fully aware of this country's shameful history, as well as our ongoing struggles with racism and prejudice. Come Election Day, I may well be disappointed in my fellow citizens if the color of his skin stops some people from selecting his name on a ballot. But if there is anything I have learned from Barack Obama, it is the power, yes, the audacity of hope.

Let's take that hope for a spin.

11

The Promise for Progress

o o o o o o o o o o o o o o o o o o o o o o o o o o o o o o o o o o

Henry Kraemer is a native of the Pacific Northwest and serves as College Media Liaison for Students for Barack Obama. Currently in his sophomore year at Portland State University, he sees a coming political age of social acceptance and economic rationality. He hungers to work in the sort of government Senator Obama represents.

Deep within the foundations of America lies a voice. The voice of the voter. The voice of the citizen. My father's voice. My mother's voice. Your voice and mine. It drives the process. It is politics. It is America and it has been forgotten.

Today's politicians sit isolated in the Capitol or the Statehouse, concerned mainly with reelection and the news cycle. They create more photo ops than legislation. Their minds have strayed from the voter, looking instead to cash and the party line. These men and women are not corrupt so much as removed. Removed from the average American. Removed from the empty dinner table. Removed from the domineering debt. Removed from the sick and the struggling. Too many days have passed since they took part in the small triumphs and trials of the working day. Seldom do they see the true America.

Few politicians transcend the divide. But some remain, who care for the people, who both listen and lead, truly serving not just special interests and big donors but the whole nation. We need more conscientiousness in government, more candor and more courage to do what's right.

We need Barack Obama.

Barack Obama holds the promise for progress, the possibility to put our government, our policy and our way of life back on track.

Our government has veered from its Constitution lately, discarding our essential virtues, compromising our morality for the sake of deceptive sound bites. But Barack Obama stood in defense of our freedoms. He stood in defense of habeas corpus, one of our most essential civil liberties. He stood in defense of equal rights, opposing the Federal Marriage Amendment, affirming the fact that every law-abiding American deserves every freedom and protection of the government. He stood in defense of voting rights; making sure than in an age of electoral improprieties every eligible voter gets a voice. He stood in defense of veteran's rights, giving America's finest the respect and helping hand they deserve. He stood in defense of immigrant's rights, acknowledging both the necessity of new labor and the moral mandate to give the next generation of immigrants a shot at the American dream.

Obama reaches beyond these basic—though fundamental—reforms. He not only protects the rights entrusted to us by our forefathers, he ensures new possibilities for the future. No legislator has shown more concern for America's youth than Barack Obama. America's future lies in the hands of America's students and Obama has fought to make their education as effective and affordable as possible. His first bill in the U.S. Senate, a major expansion of student aid dubbed the HOPE Act, proved his devotion to education. His Innovation Districts, which will bring cutting-edge technology and stronger teachers to struggling schools, promise a better start for every child. His ideas to extend school hours, broaden summer school programs and enact comprehensive teacher evaluation show originality and a willingness to make hard decisions for the betterment of American students.

Our future depends not simply on the health of our education system but on the health of our planet itself. While other legislators dawdled and danced around the problem of global warming, Senator Obama took the lead. He introduced many of the first major fuel reforms to take strides toward energy independence and environmental sustainability. They urge energy providers to move away from oil, encourage automotive companies to create fuel-efficient vehicles and ease the transition to alternative energy for the average American. Obama worked to expand the use of biofuels and cut away oil's influence on the American economy. As he leads us into the future, he will keep our environment stable and our economy strong.

Today's economy is working, but not for everybody. It benefits many, but hardly all. A huge slice of the population remains absent from the American economic discussion. While the financial elite sings the praises of a booming economy, working poor and middle class families go unaided and unseen. Senator

Obama sees this inequity and has created plans to help struggling families and reward the American worker. He put forward legislation to expand the Earned Income Tax Credit and Child Tax Credit. He created a plan to help lower-income workers climb the economic ladder, through training and transitional jobs. He fought to raise the minimum wage while keeping prices down. He has sought and found a way to improve the lives of average Americans and will continue to until all of us have an equal shot at success.

When we look at American life today, not everyone gets seen. Thousands upon thousands of our brave brothers and sisters are stuck in an ill-planned, ill-executed war in Iraq. Senator Obama opposed the war in 2002 and still opposes it today. Unlike other candidates, he doesn't let polling data determine his position. He predicted the disastrous outcome of the invasion, and spoke out against it. Now politicians have started to follow his lead but instead of working to end the war, they hold press conferences and propose symbolic legislation. They seem less interested in ending the war than in keeping their approval ratings high. Only Obama has taken real action. He forged legislation to put pressure on the Iraqi government and to take our troops out of Iraq by 2008. He calls for a responsible, lasting end to the war. Obama is the anti-Iraq candidate, no matter how many others jump on the bandwagon. He has been against Iraq since its beginning and he will show us its end.

I'm tired of a government unconcerned with facts, unconcerned with regular people and unconcerned with the future. I'm tired of a government more interested in sound bites than in human lives and freedoms. I'm tired of a government that cares more about beating political opposition than about improving American lives. I'm tired of a government that ignores us. I'm tired of the same old tricks and lies. And I'm tired of being tired of it. It's time to change. It's time to fix this broken system. It's time to put someone in office who will work thoughtfully and pragmatically, inclusively and insightfully, fairly and firmly. It's time for President Barack Obama.

12

A New Generation of Politics

○ ○

Joshua Gorman lives in Washington, D.C. where he is a student at George Mason University. He serves as Chief Strategist for Barack the Youth Vote and has been involved with creating and sustaining youth movements locally, nationally, and globally. One of his current projects is working with Reuniting America to pioneer a new generation of politics by bringing high-level youth leaders together from across the political spectrum to engage in transformative dialogue.

A new generation is coming of age on America's political stage, and as we awaken to a politics that is rife with partisan warfare, dominated by special interests, and controlled by leaders who are morally corrupt, it's no surprise that we are a generation that is deeply cynical and disengaged. Most of today's young Americans want nothing to do with our broken political inheritance: a two-party system that is bitterly polarized and a government that has been overrun by big-money interests and a powerful few. What ever happened to a government of the people, by the people, and for the people? Where are all the great American leaders of honor, truth, courage, and integrity? Politics today doesn't turn us on and inspire us to engage in the great project of democracy; it turns us off, renders us powerless, and fills us with apathy.

Enter a young and unexpected politician by the name of Barack Obama onto the national political stage. Ever since his electrifying keynote address at the 2004 Democratic National Convention I had been hearing all this hype about a rising new political star, a man that some were championing as "the hope of our generation" and "the future of our nation." After months of resistance and fighting off the pressure from others to check him out, one day I finally decided to watch one of his speeches online to see what all the hoopla regarding this "national savior" was all about.

Obama was addressing an audience in New Hampshire and the crowd was wild and fired up as ever. As he took the stage and people finally quieted down, he began to speak with a slow and confident cadence. It was obvious that Senator Obama was a smoothly polished politician, one who knew how to skillfully work his audience and deliver a well-crafted speech. After thanking the organizers of the event and making the usual opening comments, he began to talk in a very direct and earnest manner about the current state of American politics. As he spoke you could feel his genuine care and concern—a far cry from the usual empty rhetoric—and within those first minutes of listening to his heart-felt words, it was clear to me that Barack Obama was a different kind of politician.

As I continued to listen and be drawn in, it wasn't simply his words that were so moving and compelling, it was the contagious spirit that lived within them. It was that inescapable authenticity within his voice that makes you believe every word he said, that passion and integrity that fills you with such immense hope that one can not help but believe a better world is possible. He spoke of our need to come together as common Americans beyond partisan divides, of the stake every American has in determining the future of our country, and how all of us have it in our power to choose our national destiny. As he closed his speech and the crowd lit up in an uproarious applause, I found myself feeling deeply moved and altered. Barack Obama had awakened something vital within me, and as I would soon discover, a whole generation was awakening right alongside me.

From that point on I began to listen closely to the message Senator Obama was sharing with America. Still distrustful and holding on to lingering doubts, I wanted to make sure that Obama was the "real deal," that he was more than just a political charmer of good looks, passion, and charisma. As I read his books, watched his many speeches, and learned about his own personal story, I began to discover that he is not very different than the rest of us. Like so many Americans who have become cynical and disillusioned with our political system, Senator Obama recognizes deeply that our nation is in need of a new kind of politics. "What's troubling," he often confesses, "is the gap between the magnitude of our challenges and the smallness of our politics." Rather than giving up the fight though, Obama has found the incredible "audacity to hope" in the face of a mountain of obstacles and discouraging prospects. He has summoned forth the courage to believe that we have the power to come together and transform our nation, and as he campaigns for the Presidency of the United States of America, he is calling on us all to join with him in that cause.

For the first time ever in our generation, young people actually have a politician to vote *for* as opposed to someone to vote *against*. For the first time ever in our generation, we have a politician that we can actually look up to, admire, and revere. In Barack Obama we have found a leader with strong principles, deep convictions, and an uncompromising integrity, and today he is joining the ranks of those great Americans who have filled an entire people with hope and inspired them to action. "This is our time!" he declares. "A new generation is preparing to lead, and we're all a part of it!" Obama understands that change on the scale that the 21st century is calling for cannot be made by the heroic efforts of one man alone; it is going to take an entire nation, each and every one of us.

While many recognize that Barack Obama represents a new generation of American leadership, few understand that the dynamic force behind his successful leadership is a radically new generation of politics. "It's not enough to just change the players," claims Obama. "We have to change the game." The politics of old—partisan gridlock, slash-and-burn, destructive culture wars, immoral leadership, and ideological narrow-mindedness—must give way to the politics of new—civility, mutual respect, cooperation, ethical leadership, and a rich and open dialogue. As Senator Obama shared with thousands of students at a rally at George Mason University, what we need in the world today is "a politics that transcends and brings people together." Only such a politics will allow us to rise beyond our narrow partisan views so that we can find practical and commonsense solutions to our generation's challenges. Not only does it have the incredible power to bring forth breakthrough policy-solutions, it has the power to restore the moral character of our nation and to enliven the spirit of our democracy.

Make no doubt about it: Barack Obama is a once-in-a-generation's lifetime politician, and his run for presidency of the United States of America will be a once-in-a-nation's lifetime campaign. As he rallies our generation to join in the project of national renewal, young people are engaging in democracy and the political process like never before. Obama's youthroots movement promises to be the most massive and energetic in all of American history, and there can be little doubt that the number of new young voters he will bring to the polls in 2008 will break every existing record.

As our generation comes of age at an unprecedented crossroads in America history, we have found a rare and exceptional leader who is inspiring us to meet our nation's challenges with a bold and audacious movement of hope, courage, and positive action. He reminds us that, "Each generation is beckoned anew, to fight for what is right, to strive for what is just, and to find within itself the spirit, the sense of purpose, that can remake a nation and transform a world." This is our time. Barack Obama is leading the way. And a new generation of politics is storming the world's stage!

13

Cynicism and Hope

° °

Michael Heinz is a student at the State University of New York at Stony Brook emphasizing in political science.

"Do we participate in a politics of cynicism or do we participate in a politics of hope?"

It was when I came across that line that I knew we had something special on our hands. It was spoken by then-state Senator Barack Obama of Illinois, in his now famous speech, "The Audacity of Hope," given as the keynote address at the 2004 Democratic National Convention.

This essay is meant to be a personal response to the question, "Why Obama?"

So as I sat down to write I reflected on what really drew me to Senator Obama's message. A personal struggle with depression has led me to see the world through a veil of acrimony. However, it is in Senator Obama's words that I honestly find inspiration and, yes, hope. It is his call for the restoration of the American faith—that no matter what may lie before us, no matter how insurmountable the obstacles may seem, anyone with a love for this great country can see wrongs righted, can see justice handed down, and can see the nation transformed for the better, that leads me to believe he is indeed what we all need in the next President of the United States.

The place I currently find myself is exactly the same place Barack Obama wants to lead the country out of. Diagnosed with clinical depression a little over a year ago, I have become increasingly apathetic and counterproductive.

After first confronting this illness in my final months of high school, I thought I had found something to pull me out from under the suffocation. College, particularly my field of choice, political science, provided me with a new enthusiasm. I had always enjoyed learning about history in high school, and now that my education could be concentrated into a social science that I had come to love, I figured that I would eventually work myself out of the binding cynicism that was holding me back.

Unfortunately, the laziness returned. The melancholia prevailed. Up until very recently, I had given in to it, and let myself go both emotionally and intellectually. This past winter has brought change, however, through reflection and realization over what needs to be done to revitalize my life into something productive, meaningful, and satisfying. In short, I needed hope.

This is precisely what I believe Senator Obama intends to curb in American society. For six years now, we have been stuck in a state of politics ripe with cynicism and counterproductive ways that only hamper the progress of this great nation. Just as my personal status would waver, better one week, worse the next, the young amateur politico in me would grow frustrated with the way the country was being handled at home and abroad. The disappointment each generation has felt for the previous one since the end of the work by the Greatest Generation in World War II has only been amplified by the state of our politics and our society since the turn of the century. It is this disillusionment that has allowed for such a sorry situation to develop in America today.

Evidence for such an impaired society can be seen everywhere, everyday, in both the people that make up our government and the media that covers them. The Information Age of human history has given way to mass media more powerful than ever before. We get our news headlines from media conglomerates, which turn seven minutes of hard news each day into 24 hours of agenda-setting "infotainment," where politicians are only as grand as their sound byte, the pundit with the loudest voice wins, and reality TV reigns supreme. We have preoccupied ourselves with the mundane to the extent that we have blinded ourselves from what is really important. A good portion of my generation actually claims to get their news from a satirical comedy show on basic cable!

Our leaders themselves are not innocent in the creation of the political-media climate that exists today. Many have allowed themselves to be bought out by those with true access, those with the money at their disposal, the lobbyists and well-funded special-interest groups, only contributing to the growing and disturbing amount of money flowing into government. When we hear a member of congress say that electing candidates not of a certain religion is sinful, when we hear an administration official criticize all those who dissent as "confused," when we hear one side of the aisle criticizing the other as in support of the enemy during a time of war, it is all of us that suffer. We all suffer under the politics of division and fear.

It is Barack Obama who is one of the few currently in power who seeks not just to "end the status quo" as you hear in so many campaign promises each election year, but to genuinely transform the nation. To generate change from the bottom up, not just in government, but in society, in how people see their government and their leaders, and how they see their role as a citizen in the United States of America.

It is Barack Obama who has set forth to transcend this Red State/Blue State divide that we have drilled into our minds every even-numbered year. It is Barack Obama who would like to see the division, and the fear, and the petty nature of our politics done away with. This is the message that has not only inspired me on a personal level, but has also reinvigorated civic pride within me. It is a message that was unleashed in 2004 with these words: "Hope in the face of difficulty. Hope in the face of uncertainty. The audacity of hope! In the end, that is God's greatest gift to us, the bedrock of this nation. A belief in things not seen. A belief that there are better days ahead." It is a call for hope, a call to action that at this point feels virtually undeniable. It is this battle for hope over cynicism which we must fight for in order to answer the call made on an early February morning in Springfield, Illinois: "Let's be the generation that makes future generations proud of what we did here."

14

Time for the Future

o o o o o o o o o o o o o o o o o o o o o o o o o o o o o o o o o o

Matthew Kugler currently lives in Lawrence, Kansas where he is a sophomore majoring in Political Science at the University of Kansas. He has dedicated much of his life to charitable organizations, including the Make-A-Wish foundation, 65-Roses (CF Foundation), and as a Local Youth Representative for LifeGift (Organ Donor Organization).

A change is due. We are at a turning point in this country's history. On November 4th, 2008, millions of Americans will go to the voting booth and take part in deciding the 44th President of the United States of America. Some will vote with their traditions and religious views in mind, some will vote with morals at their side, and others will simply vote for their appropriate party. For a few, however, like myself, our vote will not be a vote for traditions, religious views, race, background, or political affiliations. It will be a vote for something much more important at stake here. It will be a vote for our future.

For my generation, the time to rise up and take action is now. The time for us to take control of our future and the future of our children, and their children is now. The time for us to end the war in Iraq and for our troops to return to the open arms of loved ones is now. The time when we take back the funding for the war and return it to our education system is now. The time when a clinic worker in the inner city and suburbs no longer has to ask a patient, "Do you have insurance?" is now. The time when our generation no longer hesitates to take control out of fear or insecurity for ourselves is now. The time when we need a leader who understands our concerns is now. The time for Barack Obama is now.

At the Democratic National Convention in 2004, many Americans got their first look at the young Illinois state senator who was looking for an open seat in the U.S. Senate. His speech gained overwhelming attention and praise and as the buzz surrounding him continued to rise, more and more questions were focused on his persona, and not the election.

Who is he? Where did he come from? Is he for real?

The hype that continued to surround Obama and helped lead him to a land-slide win for a Senate seat in 2004 was partly due to the hopelessness and lack of appeal for the presidential campaign. The lack of support for Democratic nomi-nee John Kerry and growing disdain for President George W. Bush was just a sign that for another four years the country would be divided into red states and blue states. Whoever this guy was, we'd have to wait, but wait for what?

The problems we were already facing—the War on Terror, the war in Iraq and Afghanistan, military spending, abortion rights, stem-cell research, educa-tional funding, alternative energy sources, immigration, Social Security, Medi-care/Medicaid, same sex marriage—would continue to "stay the course." It seemed easy to ignore these issues, easy at least for the Bush Administration and the GOP running Congress. The only thing they couldn't seem to ignore was the increase in imports that we received: the 1,000, then 1,500, then 2,000, and then 3,500 of our soldiers returning home in body bags. The mission wasn't accom-plished; we weren't winning. The nation was more than just divided by the color of our states; it was looking more and more like the beginning of a civil war.

You try and go on with your life, go through the routines, hoping you'll get word on the news or from a peer that the end has come—the end of the war, of the administration, of selective health care—only realizing that the calendar and time have become the enemy. The days that pass have become our terrorists. They have us feeling unsafe in our homeland. Is this what our generation's legacy will be?

Franklin D. Roosevelt said in his 1932 Inaugural Address, "The only thing we have to fear is fear itself." Yet the Bush administration has thrived off and built their entire second term on keeping us in a constant state of fear. An ever-chang-ing color chart informs us of the day's forecast. Will it be peaceful? Is an attack coming? From where? We don't know. From who? We don't know. And when? We're not quite sure.

Who voted for this? What happened to the government that worked for the people? What happened to our allies? What happened to America?

I've since focused on why our country is in such disarray, what exactly is going on in the administration and in congress that gives me and many other young Americans an unsettling look into the bleak future that we'll be responsible for. If only there was someone we had forgotten we were waiting on, someone that could give us hope, light for the future, someone that had been working from the inside all this time, someone who had heard our cries for a change and was working on breaking the trend, someone who could be the leader we had dreamed for since JFK, RFK, and Dr. King left us with their dream seemingly out of reach.

With Barack Obama, it seems, we finally have the potential to reclaim that dream.

Barack Obama has thus far endured the "freshman treatment" as a first-term U.S. senator. He has fought to be heard on the senate floor and is reminded again and again that he is 88th in seniority. He has learned to work with whoever he can, Republican or Democrat, in hopes of getting his bills passed. He may have had to choose which bill to push harder, knowing that you won't win them all and sometimes you have to work within the limits you're given. He has certainly gotten a look at the corruption that surrounds his profession and the unsettling requests from the lobbyists circling above. But he has pushed forward and remarkably now has a chance to be our next president.

Senator Obama understands the severity of the situation we find ourselves in and has already shown his leadership capabilities in his role as a senator. Since his induction into the Senate, he has given voice to the issues average Americans care about. As a state senator he opposed the Bush Administration's plan to go to war in Iraq, one of the very few daring enough to do so. Now, faced with the decision that the administration made, Obama has decided to tackle the issue he opposed by introducing the Iraq War De-escalation Act in January 2007. The legislation begins redeployment of U.S. forces no later than May 1, 2007, with the goal of removing all combat brigades from Iraq by March 31, 2008, a date that is consistent with the expectation of the Iraq Study Group.

In changing the political system, he worked closely to draft and pass the Federal Funding Accountability and Transparency Act, designed to "create a user-friendly website to search all government contracts, grants, earmarks, and loans, thereby opening up Federal financial transactions to public scrutiny." Obama helped lead the Senate to pass the Legislative Transparency and Accountability Act, "a comprehensive ethics and lobbying reform bill with strict bans on receiving gifts and meals from lobbyists; new rules to slow the revolving door between public and private sector service; and an end to the subsidized use of corporate jets." He sponsored The Congressional Ethics Enforcement Commission Act, a bill "that would create an outside ethics commission to receive complaints from the public on alleged ethics violations by members of Congress, staff, and lobbyists. The commission would have the authority to investigate complaints and present public findings of fact about possible violations to the House and Senate Ethics Committee and Justice Department."

The issues that will greatly affect our generation for years to come are those Obama is seeking to tackle now. The current administration simply talks about "a new national energy policy focused on improvements in technology, investments in alternative fuels, and greater efforts in conservation, efficiency, and waste reduction." Senator Obama joined with Senator Lugar to introduce the American Fuels Act to increase domestic production, distribution, and end uses of bio-fuels. As the author of the Fuel Economy Reform Act, Senator Obama has worked to gain bipartisan support for an innovative approach to raising automobile fuel efficiency standards and break two decades of inaction and deadlock on reforming fuel economy laws. With the ever-growing concern for global warming, Senator Obama believes we need to act now to reduce the emission of greenhouse gases that contribute to climate change, and acted by being an original cosponsor of the Climate Stewardship and Innovation Act, which would reduce the Nation's greenhouse gas emissions substantially enough and quickly enough between 2007 and 2050.

Regarding the very important and controversial issue of health care, insurance, Medicare and Medicaid, Senator Obama believes in instituting a universal insurance policy, where every American would receive basic coverage. Obama believes in pursuing legislative initiatives to help improve health care quality, and to improve and extend what Medicare and Medicaid covers. This federal government provided program would ensure that every American receives adequate medical care throughout their life regardless of their health status and income.

Some may wonder why all of this matters now, or why we can't just put more faith in the current system. The bottom line is the current system is not working and the problems we face are getting worse. We are at a point in this country's history where the poor and uneducated are blamed for not keeping up, even though poor school funding and lack of employment opportunities continue. We blame the elderly for living too long, requiring too many prescriptions and needing the health coverage they were guaranteed when forming this nation's economy. We divide ourselves as a nation, separating the "secular progressives" from the "traditionalists," neither of whom have made any attempts to change the system, even though their countless books, interviews, rallies, and television hosts deem that they and only they know the "answer" for what's best for America. When we're angry, confused, and hopeless about a war we can't get out of, we re-elect the man responsible for its creation to "serve us" for another four years.

Yet with all the frustration, it's time to stop complaining and take action. It's time to stop sitting idle and hoping things will eventually settle down. It's time to stop blaming those with different beliefs and traditions than ourselves for our self-created problems. It's time to stop the separation that is occurring in our nation between the rich and poor, the educated and uneducated, the young and old, the traditionalists and secularists, the liberals and the conservatives. It's time to stop the incompetence, ignorance, and uncompromising nature of our current political system. It's time to stop voting for the "lesser of two evils."

It's up to us—the future of this country—to take matters into our own hands. We can't wait anymore. We need to make the first move and we need to make it now. The first step is to choose a leader who has shown he can make changes towards progress. The time for a leader who has faith in the strength and will of the people, and to whom the people can trust is now. We need that leader who will work with us, side by side in guiding this country back to greatness. We also need to ensure that such a great leader can count on us for support. We can't do it without him, and he can't do it without us. The time to take a stand and take back our future is now.

The time for Barack Obama is now.

15

A Return of Civil Discourse

○ ○

William Figueroa is a student at Rice University in Texas where he is double-majoring in Anthropology and Chinese.

Ending partisan politics? No more "politics as usual"? The "audacity of hope"? What exactly does any of this mean?

These are some of the questions I asked myself when I first heard about Barack Obama, as people hailed him as "exactly what this country needed." But I didn't see it—how does a person end partisan politics? Americans will always disagree on issues. But with a little reading, I finally figured out what everyone was so excited about—and it wasn't what I thought at first.

I see that I previously understood what people were saying when they suggested that Obama was a bipartisan who would work to unite this country. It was not that they thought he would give conservative concessions to liberal gains, or vice versa, which is what I originally thought they were saying as was opposed to, because simply put, such a thing would be impossible—we will not be able to pay less taxes but support more people's medical bills. That wasn't it at all.

It was the mere recognition that the other side is not presenting an invalid position.

The assertion in today's politics is that those whom you are speaking against are presenting the wrong opinion. Take abortion, for example. Those who are for it are portrayed as murderers, and those against it are portrayed as religious zealots or those who would seek to take away women's rights. Is it not possible that someone support abortion not because they do not care about the rights of an unborn child, but because they care more about the well-being of a woman? Is it not possible that someone be against abortion, like myself, because they believe in the sanctity of life, and the chance of life for all people, regardless of the potential hardships (though I'm not heartless; in cases of medical emergency or extreme circumstances such as rape, I would never deny a woman her right to choose).

Or how about this thought—is it not possible that a person be personally against abortion, but respect that other people do not share their viewpoint and thus not draw up legislation to ban it?

Barack Obama seems like the type of person who would be a uniter in the sense that when people who disagreed with his opinion came along, they would not, as the current administration does, be painted as terrorists, unpatriotic, or anti-America. They would be treated as people with opposing beliefs, with whom open dialogue should commence that both sides can learn from. In the end, perhaps Obama's stance won't change—but the other side will have been given their time to speak, treated as a respected viewpoint, as another human being with an opinion and not just a labeled radical. And perhaps Obama will make an accommodation to find middle ground, or perhaps not. But hopefully his decision will be for the good of the American people.

I now understand the idea of Obama's potential to unite far more clearly. He does seem to me to be the breath of fresh air that politics needs—the departure from shouting and labeling. Perhaps it will not change much on Capitol Hill in regards to how things work and the excesses of democracy that no man can curb, but perhaps it will add some civility and intelligent discourse to the Democratic process, and the process of governing our great nation.

Should he not become president in 2008, perhaps, when he has paid his dues like so many in power and been brought to greater power himself, he will be able to do something about the rut that American Democracy has sadly fallen into.

16

A New Bus Driver

ooooooooooooooooooooooooooooooooooooo

Nathan Lean is a senior piano major at East Carolina University and the director of the online group, Rock with Barack. He is a Master's in International Studies candidate with a focus in political science and cultural arts. He has spent time living in and touring Morocco and has performed various concerts as a guest of the United States Embassy.

Perhaps it's his charisma that seems so contagious; perhaps it's the sincerity in his tone or the relevance in his message; perhaps it's the purpose in his voice that transcends generations and appeals to our common desire for innate goodness—goodness in a political system that has been distrustful and divisive. Embodying the basic principles of the American ideal and offering them with a hopeful spirit and grateful heart, Senator Barack Obama reminds us that our desires for brighter days are attainable and that America is ready for a "politics of hope."

There are times in the history of our country when the "passing of the torch" was necessary for stability and cohesion of the principles of democracy. Americans sought fresh perspectives on the issues and became disgruntled with party dominance and status-quo politics. Administrations gambled with foreign affairs and legislation, seeking to build a dominant empire of partisanship. Democracy took on a new twist when lawmakers suddenly became resolute on pushing their political envelope at the expense of their constituents. Then there was Barack Obama. A man who championed the causes of laid-off steel workers in the suburbs of Chicago, fighting for their jobs; a man who took his Harvard law degree back to the communities that helped shape his life; a man who proved to America that the little guy matters; a man who recognized the failure of an Iraq invasion long before any air strike began; someone that we can relate to.

On February 10, 2007, standing before a crowd of nearly 15,000 supporters, politics in America changed for the better. Announcing his candidacy, Obama gave America back its optimism. With the spirit of Lincoln floating around Springfield like a silent voice of approval, Barack Obama presented the people of the United States of America with the chance to have a relevant political process. This relevancy, combined with sincerity is why Barack Obama changed my mind about politics.

Proving that innate goodness and desire for a changed political process are qualities that transcend party lines, Obama combined forces with Republican Senator Tom Coburn to pass his first piece of legislation allowing citizens to view the ways their tax dollars are spent by creating an accessible online database. Working with Republican Dick Lugar, Barack Obama traveled to Russia to begin a new era of non-proliferation efforts showing the world that diplomacy is still a viable method of homeland protection and world peace. His firm intelligence is complimented by a real-world vivacity. Appearing on late night television and Super Bowl commercials, Barack seems to understand that political rhetoric is a thing of the past. Explaining the situation in Iraq to Conan O'Brien, Obama related Bush policy to driving a bus into the ditch. First, we must get the bus out of the ditch, then we need to fire the driver. The following day, videos of the interview skyrocketed on YouTube as young voters eager for a politician they could relate to downloaded clips.

I can't help but remember with a smile, the photographs and stories of events I only dreamed of attending. One event in particular proved to me that my inclinations about Obama and his relevancy are correct. At a recent rally, thousands of people flocked to shake hands with the man that changed this process. Eager for a signature, photograph, or handshake, they waited anxiously in the cold weather. Told that there was no way to access the fans, Barack Obama, in a sharply pressed black suit and slacks, took off his sunglasses, put down his water bottle, and crawled underneath the steel-framed bleachers making his way through the dirt and dust into the crowd where he stood for nearly an hour making sure each person had a chance to meet their hero. It's as if the laid-off steel plant workers in Chicago so many years ago were whispering: "It's safe to climb under here Barack. You helped us build these bleachers with your faith in our abilities."

The time for "a politics of hope" is now. We need a leader that understands our generation. We need a political process that answers to the people that helped create it. We need a relevant voice in the White House. We need a hope-based vision for our future. We need Barack Obama.

17

Practical Idealist

∘ ∘

Teresa Lynn Brecht was born in Hutchinson, Minnesota and is currently an undergraduate physics student at the University of Minnesota. She strives to include politics and community organizing as a significant and gratifying part of her life.

In the early stages of the 2006 governor's race in Minnesota, I was attracted to the optimistic and idealistic candidate because of the hope aroused in my youthful spirit. Ultimately, however, I felt compelled to vote for the candidate that was more practical and, unfortunately, more like a "regular politician" because I knew he had a better chance of winning the election. It is unfortunate that in that race and many others, voters are forced into the predicament of choosing between an "idealistic" and a "practical" candidate. In the 2008 presidential race, we finally have an opportunity to choose a candidate possessing both the optimistic vision of an idealist and the rationality of a pragmatic politician. Barack Obama is ready to seize the opportunity and satisfy America's hunger for a president capable of facilitating workable plans to achieve idealistic goals. He is both America's idealistic and practical choice for president in 2008.

Many Americans are pessimistic about the future of America because of the corruption and unresponsiveness of our public officials that seem to be ingrained in the system of government itself. While in the legislature, Obama saw much of this corruption in the form of scandals, special interests, pork barrel spending, and partisan pressure. He found these vices discouraging and unrewarding, but did not give up hope or settle for weak and superficial fixes. He spearheaded the effort to clean up Washington by contributing the most sweeping parts of ethics legislation.

America began a fresh start in the 2006 election be replacing some Republican incumbents, but that was just the beginning and means nothing without subsequent action. In an editorial for the *Washington Post*, Obama wrote, "It's not enough to just change the players. We have to change the game." Note that he is not calling for a disorderly revolution to change all precedent, but a radical reform to restore values of transparency and accountability to a level that will ensure a smooth path into the future. The White House is in desperate need of this fresh outlook.

Barack Obama has realistic and workable plans to accomplish lofty goals that most liberal politicians can only afford to speak about vaguely, as if they only existed far off on a hazy horizon. He knows that if we rise above partisan bickering to realize that we are all in this together, we have the ability to foster positive change. As one American family, we all agree that we want to better educate our youth, better care for our sick and elderly, increase our security in a changing world, build a more competitive economy and become more energy independent. We can achieve these things with smart government built on consensus.

Obama will not be satisfied with just being a leader; he will work to be a leader with renowned domestic support and international respect. At a time of plummeting presidential approval ratings and steadily declining support in the world, we cannot afford to select an ordinary politician. I have already observed Obama's power to connect with and inspire people. My friends and relatives normally disinterested or repelled by politics are beginning to talk about him energetically. Ordinary people are interested in donating both money and volunteer time to be a part of the Obama movement, many for the first time. It is extremely inspiring to see formerly apathetic people becoming engaged citizens behind grassroots efforts supporting an original candidate.

Obama will reclaim the hope of a discouraged country, build consensus on clear objectives, and lead responsibly. He offers more than just an optimistic view of the future. He demonstrates an understanding of the current issues we face as a country and offers practical ways to move forward. I am supporting Barack Obama for president in 2008 because he is both idealistic and practical.

18

The Real Thing

o o o o o o o o o o o o o o o o o o o o o o o o o o o o o o o o

Shannon Craig is a graduate of Neuqua Valley High School in Naperville, Illinois. She now attends Hope College in Holland, Michigan as a Political Science and History double major. Shannon currently serves as the Michigan Field Director of Students for Barack Obama.

I wanted to tell some grand narrative explaining my support for Senator Obama, but soon realized there isn't one speech, one event, or one issue that drives my passion. I can't write a majestic account of my support for Obama because there isn't one. Obama is simply the real thing.

In his story, I can see myself. In his writing, I see the values my mother instilled in me. In his speeches, I see the principles I believe will make this country great again.

I remember seeing Senator Obama at a town hall meeting at Addison Trails High School during my senior year of high school. I had received special permission to leave graduation practice early after a member of my church who served on the county board invited me to attend the town hall meeting with him. The audience was a mix of retirees and high school students, men and women, black and white. No matter who asked a question, the senator afforded everyone the same great respect. He didn't distinguish between those who were old enough to vote and those who weren't. He didn't gloss over the questions of the younger members of the audience. Everyone there mattered to him.

Senator Obama has time and time again reminded America of what he calls "the audacity of hope." I had the opportunity to hear the Senator announce his candidacy for President at the Old State Capitol building in Springfield, Illinois. That cold February day he asked us to remember that hope calls us to take action, to give our time to make even the smallest difference, to stand before Goliath with only a sling and a few stones. I will never forget how I felt listening to this simple but profound message.

As a college student, I am searching for my place in the world. I wonder if my life will matter and where my hope will lead me. Will I have the courage to hope even when things seem grim? Will I be able to stand, like David before Goliath, in front of a world that tells me I cannot succeed? Will I play a role in helping this country realize its potential? I have learned to believe again because of Senator Obama and his promise, in bleak times, of better days for our country.

19

The Content of his Character

○ ○

Caseen Gaines is a student at Rutgers University, where she is studying American Studies, English, and Journalism.

I remember the day I first felt myself really getting into politics. It was a summer day in 2004, the day after Michael Moore's *Fahrenheit 9/11* opened. As I watched the film in Paramus, New Jersey, with a packed audience, I sat stunned and silent until the end credits. As I was leaving the theater, I thought out loud to a stranger who happened to be near me, "There's no way George W. Bush is going to be re-elected."

I believed this from before the 2004 Democratic National Convention through election night. I believed this until Florida was called for Bush by a sizable (though questionable) margin, with Ohio appearing to go that way as well. In spite of everything—John Kerry's alleged "flip-flopping," the Swift Boat veterans ads, the fact that no incumbent president had ever lost re-election during a time of war, and Kerry's infamous "I actually did vote for the $87 billion before I voted against it"—I still believed that change would come in this country. I had, quite simply, the audacity to hope in spite of everything else.

But on that election night, my hope subsided. As I watched Wolf Blitzer color Ohio green, a makeshift mixture of red and blue to state that Ohio was "too close to call," I clicked through the channels and found that Fox News had declared Bush the winner. I felt defeated. I was personally destroyed. John Edwards took to the stage around 2 in the morning to announce that he and Kerry would not rest until every vote was counted, but I couldn't help but see him as a liar; a well-meaning parent who protects his child's feelings by saying Santa Claus exists when his child is filled with doubt. As Bush was sworn in, with a solemn Kerry looking on, I was more fearful than hopeful about the future of the war, the polarization of our country, the well-being of America.

That was until Senator Barack Obama announced on Meet the Press that he was considering running for president. I was familiar with Obama since before his DNC Speech in 2004. I considered him a political enigma even then—someone who did not seem to fit into the stereotype of the slimy politicians that I had become accustomed to, but still got a fair amount of media attention. After his announcement and subsequent *Time* Magazine cover story, I decided to do some research on this person the pundits described as a "political rock star," a term that I personally find condescending and dismissive of his ability.

Obama instantly impressed me. Obama was the first black president of the *Harvard Law Review*. He succeeded rapidly in his career through self-motivation and the support of his wife, not by being involved in dirty politics or having a last name instantly recognizable to voters like Bush or Clinton. As a community organizer in Illinois, he strengthened inner-cities and worked diligently within low-income communities to help them prosper, not because of the color of their skin, but because he understood that a chain is only a strong as its weakest link. In 2002, he publicly opposed the Iraq War, with arguably less information than Senators John Edwards and Hillary Clinton, who initially supported the war.

With his impressive resume, charismatic personality, and intriguing personal history, I can't help but find myself inspired by Obama. His life story is amazingly emblematic of the "great American melting pot." One of the things I hear most frequently from Obama detractors is that he's inexperienced and has no opinion on issues, but that is more a reflection of media coverage than reality. He worked diligently to gain bi-partisan support in the Illinois state senate and has been commended for his hard work in the United States senate by both Democrats and Republicans. The media seems more fixated talking about the size of his crowds than the content of his speeches.

I support Obama because he has allowed me to hope again. In spite of the Iraq War escalation, a possible war with Iran and/or North Korea on the horizon, and a still-corrupt government that seems desperate to destroy our rights as Americans, I believe that we can, and will, do better. Obama challenges all of us to cast aside our cynicism and take responsibility for ourselves. While he does have a number of high-profile financial supporters, his grassroots-style campaign is largely supported by ordinary people. When I donated to his campaign, my first time donating to any presidential candidate, I felt like I had made an important investment into my future. Whether or not Obama wins, his influence on me and millions of others will be permanent. Many of us have been inspired by

Obama and look forward to doing all we can to ensure that he is elected President of the United States in November of 2008.

20

Hope and Renewal

o o o o o o o o o o o o o o o o o o o o o o o o o o o o o o o o o o o o

Joseph Seago was born in California, raised in Colorado, and currently lives in New York City where he is studying Political Science at York College of the City University of New York. An active, passionate and proud Democrat since childhood, Joseph currently focuses on disability issues and press/communications for both the College Democrats of America and the Young Democrats of America. Aside from being a statewide and national leader in college politics, Joseph is also an avid writer and blogger for Campus Progress.

Like many of my fellow college students, my political journey was sparked by hope. As a young boy, I watched the glowing images of practical idealism on my television screen long before I fully understood their context or meaning. Long before I grasped the differences between Democrats and Republicans, I felt the sustaining power of hope and renewal in the moving words that filled my eager ears. The inspiring, patriotic image of then Governor Bill Clinton accepting his party's nomination for President of the United States left an indelible impression. That was the first political memory I formed, a memory formed when I was much too young to understand the dynamics of my country's political structure.

When I was introduced to Senator Barack Obama with the rest of the nation in July of 2004 at the Democratic National Convention, the sense of sustaining power again rushed through me as he spoke of a "belief that we are connected as one people." I felt inspired and proud to be an American as I watched Obama's keynote address. He seemed to embody something our country desperately needed.

As a white male of mixed European origin I do not posses the dark skin of Barack Obama. But that does not mean I haven't intimately felt the sting of discrimination for being "different." I may not have bloodlines to Jim Crow's casualties yet that does not prevent me from knowing the face of bigotry and prejudice. To the casual observer I may personify "WASP" culture: a privileged stranger to the lessons of fortitude and perseverance taught by the teachers of struggle and pain. The reality is that with a series of birth defects, my story is also one of struggle, pain, and discrimination. However, it is also one of hard-earned strength and optimism.

I was born with Pierre Robin syndrome, which gave me an exceptionally short jaw and a cleft palate, a combination resulting in a speech impediment I will carry with me to my grave. Additional birth defects caused a commotion of complications at birth, compromising my chance at life. After I won my first of many life-long battles in the beginning hours of my existence, doctors told my parents that I would not be able to engage in normal childhood activities like my peers (many of whom would later show me the face of discrimination and prejudice on the playground).

I faced struggle and pain and even the temptation of cynicism; yet I gained strength in compassion, strength in relating to others as fellow human beings engaged in their own personal struggles. Instead of cynicism I chose hope. Instead of conceding to doubters who told me I wouldn't be able to use my God-given talent for speech and prose, I told them "Yes, I can." I am now the state-wide Communications Director of the College Democrats of New York and the national Vice-Chair of the Disability Caucus of the College Democrats of America—evidence of what Barack Obama so commonly refers to as the "audacity of hope."

Like all past Americans who have fought and worked to attain their dreams, every American today has a story. Every citizen can recant their own magnificent mixture of triumph and tragedy through the inevitable pain and struggle that accompanies an individual life. The universal attributes of these hardships manifest themselves in the underpaid teacher in New York City dedicated to educating our nation's future in an impoverished inner-city environment that produces more inmates than graduates. They are demonstrated by the recently graduated woman in Colorado who must compromise her life essentials because her unpaid student loans prevent her from affording adequate health insurance. The universal face of pain surfaces in grief when a California mother learns that her only son won't be returning home because her government sent the brave soldier overseas to fight in a war initiated on false, ideological grounds and perpetuated without an exit strategy. Each of these people and millions more aren't looking for mere handouts; they're looking for hope.

Barack Obama's principles, values and life experiences, so eloquently outlined in his books, give him the moral courage to fight to fulfill the promises of our Forefathers: unfettered justice and equal opportunity for all Americans.

As a member of the Senate Health, Education, Labor and Pensions Committee, Senator Barack Obama has introduced several bills that ensure good schools through sound structural reform and adequate resources. Obama has innovated new means of increasing teacher pay, expanded summer learning opportunities, and increased access to federal college loans.4

Barack Obama believes that as one of the wealthiest nations in the world, there is no excuse for more than 46 million Americans to live without health insurance. Senator Obama is dedicated to empowering health care consumers with hospital report cards and harnessing the power of genetic medicine. He is dedicated to updating technology in the health care industry. That is exactly why "Senator Obama worked with Senator Harry Reid (D-Nevada) to introduce the Federal Employees Health Benefits Program Efficiency Act to leverage the federal government's purchasing power to encourage the development of health information technology. The bill would require medical insurance companies that deal with the federal government to implement an electronic system for efficient and effective settlement of medical claims."

Whether reaching across the aisle to help keep weapons out of the hands of terrorists or ending the ill-conceived and incompetently-executed Iraq War by surging political and diplomatic efforts in the Middle East, Senator Obama is dedicated to attacking real threats and stabilizing volatile regions in a dangerous world. Senator Obama worked with Senator Dick Lugar (R-Indiana) to introduce "comprehensive legislation to expand the cooperative threat reduction concept to conventional weapons" and "expand the detection and interdiction of weapons and materials of mass destruction." Barack Obama not only courageously spoke out against the war in 2002 when it was unpopular to do so but he restored responsibility and reason to our federal government when he called for strategic troop redeployment that will address relevant threats in the global War on Terror and "pressure the Iraqis to finally reach a political settlement and reduce the violence."

As a member of the disability community and a grandson of a decorated World War II veteran, I take notice when Barack Obama leads efforts to correct the gap between the disability benefits veterans of Illinois were receiving and the benefits bestowed upon veterans elsewhere in the country. "As a result of his efforts, VA opened an investigation into the matter, agreed to hire more disability claims specialists for the Chicago regional office and agreed to re-examine the claims of Illinois veterans who felt they had been treated unfairly." While the old ways of Washington gave us the disgrace and atrocities of Walter Reed's degradation, the vision and action of Barack Obama reveal a new kind of politics. It reveals a man that cares enough about our active soldiers and veterans that they are properly taken care of by the country they served with such courage and sacrifice.

Barack Obama will be the first to admit that his unlikely run for president carries a degree of presumptuousness. He understands there is a strong sense of audacity for someone so young and so new to Washington to tell the American people he is ready to lead the Free World. Detractors commonly say that Obama lacks the experience necessary to serve as President of the United States. I am not entirely sure what comprises their presidential litmus test for experience, but history—the history of my generation and the history of generations before me—tells me Barack Obama stands on solid ground when he says he has "been [in our nation's capitol] long enough to know that the ways of Washington must change."

It was in the heat of slavery's hellish grip on divided Americans that an experienced politician became one of the worst presidents in United States history. Ten years in the U.S. House of Representatives, ten years in the U.S. Senate, two-time United States ambassador to London and Moscow and four years served as Secretary of State still did not give James Buchanan enough experience to effectively serve as Commander-in-Chief. Virtually no one—Democrat or Republican—disputes the gross failure that was Buchanan's administration. Yet too many skeptics believe previous political experience serves as a sufficient indicator of future presidential success.

Abraham Lincoln's skimpy pre-presidential experience certainly was enough to give him the ability to unite a divided country haunted by civil war. Robert Kennedy certainly had enough pre-presidential experience as a first-term Senator to inspire Americans to action in order to begin healing the racial tensions and wounds inflicted by Vietnam and to ultimately rise above politics and unite as fellow Americans and fellow human beings.

In contrast to an out-of-touch Head of State who fails to strong-arm a red-tape-infested federal government to help poor citizens of New Orleans drowning in Third World living conditions, Barack Obama offers grassroots experience as a former community organizer. This position allowed Obama to personally make a difference in the heart of despair and connect with citizens trapped in desolation.

In contrast to the gutting of civil rights and liberties in the name of security and unconstitutionally wiretapping American citizens, Barack Obama offers experience as a well-respected Constitutional scholar and fierce civil rights lawyer who taught Constitutional Law at the University of Chicago. In contrast to the sheltered philosophy of a president who barely traveled abroad before occupying the Oval Office, Barack Obama offers experience in living abroad, studying, breathing and connecting with cultures and history which are so vital to understand in order to successfully alleviate tensions in the Middle East and elsewhere.

No presidential candidate in the field today has the ability to draw crowds like Barack Obama because no candidate in the field today has the ability to inspire my generation like Barack Obama. Chronic political apathy among college students is not simply a product of inadequate education or skewed priorities on behalf of my generation; rather it is the product of uncompassionate and corrupt politicians with their own priorities who too often and for too long discredit my generation's stake in the country's future. My generation is the country's future and inspiring America's future to action, inspiring the nation's future to fight for a politics of hope, inspiring an entire generation to get involved in politics and speak out on America's direction is what Barack Obama is doing. He promises an American future characterized by harmonious prosperity for all Americans—black and white, young and old, rich and poor.

Every American has a story. My story can't be told without mentioning my political awakening when I visited the United States Holocaust Memorial Museum a few years ago during my first visit to the nation's capitol. A particular temporary exhibit hit a nerve so hard that it caused a dramatic rise in my personal sense of patriotism and activism that paved the road to my tireless support of Senator Barack Obama today. Browsing through an exhibit on the Nazi medical experiments, genetic engineering, and systematic torture of the disabled brought me to a graphic picture of mutilated heads of young children born with cleft lips and cleft palates-their only crime. It was at that moment that I fully realized how fortunate I was to be born in the United States, the land of the free and home of the brave where a skinny writer with a knack for public speaking and an accompanying speech impediment could thrive and contribute to society.

Senator Barack Obama's story is representative of all of our stories. His connection to our lives takes root in his own life: his experiences, his vision, his principles and his values—and that is the key to an effective president. No amount of experience gave any other candidate the brilliant foresight, keen intelligence and sound judgment that Obama had in 2002 when he publicly declared at an antiwar rally: "I don't oppose all wars. And I know that in this crowd today there is no shortage of patriots or of patriotism. What I am opposed to is a dumb war. What I am opposed to is a rash war."

Responsibly ending the Iraq War to redirect our attention to gathering threats and to stabilize the Middle East is not only part of Barack Obama's vision but a top priority. Senator Barack Obama will restore hope and renewal in this country through better schools, universal healthcare and homeland security that truly supports the troops and keeps Americans safe. My generation may be the biggest block of Obama's support, yet it is my generation, with Senator Barack Obama's leadership, that will serve as the world's hope and renew the promise of America.

I conclude with an excerpt of a speech Robert Kennedy gave in South Africa which sent forth a ripple of hope in the land of apartheid:

> Our answer is the world's hope; it is to rely on youth. The cruelties and the obstacles of this swiftly changing planet will not yield to obsolete dogmas and outworn slogans. It cannot be moved by those who cling to a present which is already dying, who prefer the illusion of security to the excitement and danger which comes with even the most peaceful progress. This world demands the qualities of youth: not a time of life but a state of mind, a temper of the will, a quality of imagination, a predominance of courage over timidity, of the appetite for adventure over the life of ease … it is the young people who must take the lead."

21

What a President Should Be

∘ ∘

Thomas Fringer is currently an undergraduate student at The College of William and Mary, in Williamsburg, Virginia, where he is pursuing degrees in Public Policy and Government. He graduated in 2006 from Westfield Senior High School, in Westfield, New Jersey. He splits his time between his home in New Jersey and college in Virginia.

I often encounter difficulty when it comes to explaining exactly why it is the case that I support Senator Obama in his bid for the Presidency. Over dinners at The Caf my friends like to both pepper me with a wide variety of questions and beseech me for numbers from polls and other statistics that justify his capabilities in comparison to other candidates. They ask me to provide examples of legislation that he has introduced to the Senate, and they always want me to point to instances in which the senator has worked directly with members of the Republican Party (he preaches bipartisanship, they say, and unless his rhetoric is empty, there must be a specific moment that you can point to where he eagerly worked with his co-workers across the aisle).

By far their favorite tactic is to claim that he is unelectable, pointing to the fact that he doesn't even have the Black vote. Enter the familiar phrase, "America is not ready for a Black president." They will then, sensing triumph, question how, given the "argument" they have just presented, I can plausibly believe that this inexperienced kid is fit to assume the office of President of the United States (that is, only when courteous enough not to attack me ad hominem for my naïveté).

As is probably evident, I am immediately put on the defensive, forced to refute a mountain of claims, which, in the end, amount to nothing more than accusations. But I believe that the quantificational analysis of a candidate is something that should be left to the pollsters, the pundits, and the media. Not only do numbers make their jobs simpler by enabling them to break down complex issues into easy-to-interpret data, but they help in supporting contrived arguments based almost wholly on speculation and inferences.

What I prefer is an analysis that acknowledges the complexity of an individual. Then, measurements of other sorts take on more importance in developing beliefs. These types of measurements are not the ones that statistics can aptly evaluate; they are the ones that are instead subject to personal judgment. They are the measurements of character. And it is according to these evaluations that Senator Obama becomes an impressive candidate.

I am a big fan of the hit drama *The West Wing*. While the show may be a mere representation of an idealistic world of politics, or a "fantasy about what the White House might be like if honor and intellectual brilliance ever trumped cupidity and mediocrity," I cannot deny that much of the content strikes a chord somewhere deep inside of me. In one episode, Communications Director Toby Ziegler remarks: "If our job teaches us anything, it's that we don't know what the next President's going to face. And if we choose someone with vision, someone with guts, someone with gravitas, who's connected to other people's lives, and cares about making them better … if we choose someone to inspire us, then we'll be able to face what comes our way and achieve things we can't imagine yet."

When I talk about character, it's this it is this type of description that I am referring to. Does Senator Obama have vision? Absolutely. It was he who knew how the Iraq War would play out way back in 2002. Does he have guts, and gravitas? Again, as evidenced by his opposition to the Iraq War, yes he does. His opposition in the face of overwhelming support for the invasion, among members of his own party and during a senatorial campaign nonetheless, is more than what can be said for 95% of his colleagues. I could go on an on, providing examples of how he fits Toby Ziegler's description of what a president should be. But what it comes down to is that the office of the president demands a whole lot of the person who wishes to occupy it.

That person has to have integrity, honesty, intelligence, and above all, he or she must be trustworthy. Senator Obama meets, and even exceeds, these standards. I am inspired by this man every single time that I hear his name on CNN, or read an article about him online. I now know that there is hope for the future of this country, and it comes in the form of this senator from the state of Illinois.

I still get chills every time I watch Senator Obama's 2004 Keynote Speech at that year's Democratic Convention. In retrospect, I can't help but feel that the speech is somewhat tinged with a flavor of irony. Who would have ever thought that this speech in support of Senator John Kerry would lead to his propulsion into the forefront of the political scene, and at least indirectly launch his bid for the Presidency?

I'll leave it up to each individual voter to evaluate each candidate according to their own terms and standards. But this is the way that I came to my decision and why my vote will be for Senator Barack Obama.

22

A True Leader

○ ○

Robby Grossman is a senior at Wheaton College in Norton, Massachusetts. In addition to majoring in Computer Science, he has focused on studying American Foreign Policy. An avid political junkie, he has experience working for county and state campaigns, including Whitehouse for Senate in 2006.

This past summer, I studied in Alaska with the National Outdoor Leadership School (NOLS). "School" is perhaps a relative term. The "semester" was certainly not the image that one conjures up of the typical three months of applied learning. We spent our days instead paddling in kayaks and hiking with backpacks, literally hundreds of miles away from the nearest classroom. But school it was, and learn I did. The outside-the-box approach that NOLS employs parallels the outside-the-box priorities and values that the school works to instill in its students: leadership, responsibility and ethics.

Leadership, responsibility and ethics: broad words with loose definitions.

In my 20 years, conventional schooling had been able to teach me neither what these words mean nor what the people whom they describe embody. I may have recognized these things when I saw them, but I surely couldn't articulate or thoroughly understand them. That ability came from NOLS, which taught me not through lectures or textbooks, but through trial-and-error and experience. I learned that these terms are not distinct, as they appear on paper, but inseparable, as they exist throughout the world. My ability to lead my group required that I fulfilled my obligations and that I did so according to a set of values that I believed to be sound.

After acknowledging this, it was only a few group discussions later that I was able to define leadership in practical, applicable and meaningful terms. A leader is somebody who helps those around him to reach their full potential. When that happens, the group reaches its collective potential and everybody stands to benefit.

On some days this meant working with our group's best navigator or map-reader to plan the following day's route. On others it meant cooking breakfast for a buddy who overslept. Sometimes it was as simple as checking in with an injured tent-mate to make sure that we were giving him enough time to nurse his injury. These actions are all mutually beneficial; helping each other helps the group at-large. These same principles extend anywhere and everywhere that leadership takes place.

There is no word that more accurately describes Illinois Senator Barack Obama than "leader." He leads not only capably, but instinctively. He has spent his entire life leading, helping those around him to reach their full potential. As a college student at Occidental he criticized the anti-intellectual movement associated with minorities, claiming that it reduces their abilities and diminishes their progress. After graduating from Columbia University, he passed on a career in business to organize minority communities and help low-income families find jobs. Wanting to do more for these people, he studied law at Harvard Law School, where he continued to lead as president of the *Harvard Law Review*. Obama stayed loyal to his cause after receiving his J.D., passing on high-income corporate opportunities to help those in his community. He empowered citizens by directing a registration drive and helped minorities in suburban Chicago by working at civil rights firm. In every place he's been and with every thing he's done, Obama has helped those around him to make the most of their lives.

Obama became officially recognized as the public servant he's always been when he was elected to the Illinois State Senate. With the same values and priorities that he'd always had, he harnessed his new power to bring tax relief to low-income families and health care to those who could not afford it. Serving in the United States Senate, Obama has worked at the national level to push America forward. He's worked to diminish employment by voting to help keep jobs in the United States. He's worked to expand education funding by voting to fund it with money that was otherwise lost in corporate tax loopholes. He's worked to force politicians to work for people rather than corporations by voting to make gifts from lobbyists to congressmen illegal and by drafting legislation that makes all meetings between congressmen and lobbyists public information. He's worked to help seniors attain medical insurance by voting to extend the deadline for enrollment in Medicare Part D. At every stage of his career, Obama has used his position and resources to help those around him. There is no better mark of a leader.

And there is no job more demanding of such a leader than that of President of the United States. It is we who must work to make this nation stronger and safer, but it is the president who must inspire us and provide us with the means to do so. The president must choose a strategy for the War in Iraq so that our troops can return safely. The president must create jobs so that we can work to pay off the national debt and save social security. The president must improve efficiency in the health care industry so that when we're sick we can recover quicker and cheaper and get right back to work.

When selecting our president, we must choose the candidate who is the most capable of leading because that is the very essence of the job. Barack Obama has proven time and time again that he can better the lives of those around him. It's time we put him in a position to work for all of America.

23

A Breath of Fresh Air

o o o o o o o o o o o o o o o o o o o o o o o o o o o o o o o o

Mark Rutledge is currently a Fellow at The Greenlining Institute in Berkeley, California where he works on increasing access to advanced information and communications technology for low-income and minority communities. Mark is a native of Detroit, Michigan, and in 2006 received his Bachelor of Arts from Eureka College (Eureka, IL) in Political Science and History, with a concentration in Communications. In his spare time Mark enjoys reading socio-political commentaries, writing lucid thoughts on life and the state, viewing Netflix films and going to the gym.

Liberty. Justice. Peace. Happiness. All ideals that many of us each day seek to achieve in our own lives and seek to help those around us reach as well. As Americans, we are each given so much and it is the least we can do to ensure that these principles of human pursuits are never left by the wayside and forgotten about. But what happens when these ideals become thought of as being unique to Americans? Even worse, when these ideals are too distant for even the majority of Americans to comprehend? What happens when the "fire" of liberty, justice, peace and happiness seems to be losing its life?

What do you do when a flame begins to die?

I have always been intrigued by the fact that no flame, no fire ever has to end. A moving breeze or a fervent breath can bring life back into a flame. Without getting into the scientific nuances of the role oxygen plays in sustaining a fire, let me just say that it is time for that moving breeze, that fervent breath to bring a renewed vibrancy to the "fire" of the American democracy. Liberty, justice, peace and happiness for all the world depends upon it.

Barack Obama is that moving breeze, and those that believe in him and the ideals he stands for, we are that fervent breath.

Our generation is coming of age during a time in this world's history where the hopes and dreams of peace, love, liberty, justice and happiness are seemingly distant and even passé. War and the threat of war loom above our heads. Communities remain divided across unnatural lines constructed solely for social means (racial, religious, gender, sexual, national, etc.). Education, even in its inaccessibility to many, has become almost solely a tool for "getting ahead" as opposed to a means to connect with one's place in the world and as a part of a global community. I found myself quite dismayed following the 2004 Presidential Election because I saw it as the one opportunity for us to move beyond these (and many other) symptoms of social regression. Backed into a proverbial corner and with my own embers of being a democratic citizen ready to die, I and many others like me were left with many questions. Where will we go from here? Who will we look to? Will we continue to move on this trajectory we have found ourselves on?

Drastic times call for drastic measures, and these are drastic times. Barack Obama to me represents the potential for a true movement, not just a presidential campaign with workers, interns and canvassers aggressively spouting out the run of the mill political rhetoric of a strategically chosen candidate. Instead, we are witnessing a man, an American, who carries our deepest hopes, dreams and beliefs both deep in his core to inform his own actions and on his sleeves in order to share it with those that look to him for leadership. With these he is fully equipped to lead a movement of Americans, particularly young Americans, that have become dismayed by the void of sound leadership that has gripped our nation since the beginning of this century, if not longer. I don't believe in campaigns any longer. We have seen them become further opportunities for elite overspending of funds that could be used to ensure health care, a quality education and comfortable shelter for every American that is currently without these. However, a movement is something that I can believe in wholeheartedly as it will not last for just an election cycle, but will be sustained in the hearts and future work of every person that is a part of it.

We each have a fire within us. When it burns it drives us to fulfill our passions in living, loving and learning. Furthermore, we achieve greater unity and connections in this world along with a greater self fulfillment when we are able to share our fire with others, especially those that have their own fire stunted by circumstances of this life. Being born into this socio-political experiment known as America gives us an ability, a privilege in fact, to draw from a torch of democracy when our own individual fires begin to weaken and lose passion and vitality. Not for our own selfish purposes but only so we can then pass that passion and vitality on to others, from our closest neighbor to our fellow human on the opposite side of the world.

Sometimes though, it takes a breath of fresh air to reinvigorate that flame of democracy. If we are left to divisive leadership and polarizing politics, that flame will surely die and we will ALL be left in darkness. Our parents and grandparents will live in fear of the world that has been created for us, their offspring. Our own children will not be properly educated and will never know what gifts they have to offer this world. The poor and often forgotten of this world will be forced to remain unheard. The marginalized will continuously be shut out and denied access to the table of power and policy. Darkness is not something we can afford to live in and it is not something we have to live in. All we need is a breath of fresh air. A breath of fresh air to reinvigorate, to breath new life, into the flame we have all come to believe in, to work for, and in some cases, even risk our life for.

Barack Obama is that breath of fresh air.

It is exhibited by the thousands of women, children and men throughout the country that have signed up online, shown up with signs at rallies, are hosting house parties and talking to their friends about this new movement that we are in the early stages of. We are all breathing that fresh air in, and, most importantly, letting it revive the fire of liberty, justice, peace and happiness that is critical to each of us fulfilling our responsibilities as conscientious participants of this American "experiment in democracy."

This is why I am a part of this movement. I myself needed a breath of fresh air in my political outlook and potential civic contributions and Barack Obama is just that. I know I am not the only one. I believe that this is more than just a campaign and that he is more than just a candidate. He is new life in this new democracy and this is a new movement for a new world.

24

Let's Get to Work

o o o o o o o o o o o o o o o o o o o o o o o o o o o o o o o o
Benjamin Weinberg is a junior at Smithtown High School West in New York. He is a member of the Political Awareness Club, Academic Quiz Bowl, secretary of the Model United Nations Club and co-founder of the Darfur Action Committee at his school. He plans to major in International Relations and Political Science in college.

I was unfamiliar with who Barack Obama was until the 2004 Democratic National Convention where he would give a stirring, powerful speech that would leave all of America yearning for more of this future bright star of the United States Senate. I did not know much about the senator then except that he was supposedly an articulate and very intelligent man who was running against conservative political activist Alan Keyes for the vacated Senate seat for Illinois. As I watched that night looking out for this potential young up and comer of the Democratic Party, I started thinking about how America could use someone who was optimistic, youthful and not corrupted or hardened by the ways of Washington. John Kerry and President George W. Bush seemed to be the two men who represented that image to me as hardened men of Washington and it made me believe that this country really needed a leader who can unite the people of this country together and lead the fight against the supposed divide between "red states" and "blue states." That night of the DNC Convention, Barack Obama delivered what I believe to be as the most inspiring speech I had ever heard from a politician during my short life. His message was appealing in that he was reaching out to every single American and he wasn't neglecting any race, religion, and ethnicity or alienating anyone's political beliefs. He appeared to be optimistic, youthful, energetic and very willing to fix the problems that continue to afflict this nation.

More than two years later, Barack Obama has exceeded the expectations that many people gave him in 2004 as he won the election for the Illinois senate seat, become an important member of the Senate and passed many laws and reforms that have made this country better because of it. He has also proven himself too many people through his words and ideas that anything is possible and that cynicism is something that we can't afford to take for granted anymore. My generation has never experienced the protests of Martin Luther King, Jr., the will and resolve of JFK to make sure that Americans do what is necessary to make their country better or the idealism and hope that Bobby Kennedy brought to Americans in his speeches and actions. You can't compare any of these historical figures to Barack Obama but you can realize that he is an embodiment of those three leaders who fought for change in America during those years of Vietnam and the Civil Rights Movement.

A person like Barack Obama does not come around every few years with a resolve for things to change or for the American people to take charge and do what is necessary to make this country the best it can be. He is a once in a lifetime figure who is in the mold of American leaders and idealists such as Lincoln and JFK. It is the enormous potential that he brings to the 2008 Presidential election that makes me believe that he is destined for greatness. Through his words and speeches, He inspires many young Americans such as myself to go out and be the change and make a difference. It is through this future generation's resolve that will decide the fate of this election and others after 2008. Every effort must be made in order for Senator Obama to become elected so that these plans and hopes for the Iraq War to end and for Universal Healthcare to be available to every American and to improve our schools and lower college tuition can and should become a reality. Politicians of the past have given us the same rhetoric and promises but this is what makes Senator Obama stands out from the rest. His words are not fake and misleading but are from the words of a man who has been with people through their tough times and who knows that every American is entitled to the same opportunities and benefits that are necessary to improve the quality of life for all people of this great nation. His charisma is also something that no other candidate of this election can mimic or recreate. He is sincere with his words and he is honest and truthful with what he believes in and how he is confident with what he knows of which beliefs and goals are possible for this country that could change it for the better and that could be achieved through the rigorous effort and hard work of this generation which needs to embrace that things don't always have to remain the same and that change is possible and must occur at times that are crucial to the legacy of a generation.

I often find myself continually checking Barack Obama's 2008 presidential campaign website. I do it usually every fifteen minutes, thinking of ways to tell fellow friends and teachers about him to spread the word and get others involved or by thinking of ways to volunteer and just be a part of this great effort to make history with people of all backgrounds working together side by side for a common effort. It's something that I would be very proud of in telling my kids one day that I helped a great man become elected to a great position. I knew from the very first speech I heard of Senator Obama's that if he were to ever run for president, he would be qualified in every way and would be ready to fulfill his duties and honor his promises. The possibilities of the things that the American people and Senator Obama can accomplish together working side by side is what really make me hopeful for the future of this nation. That is what makes this opportunity so tempting and necessary in that a person like this might never come again and I think others around the country realize this as well which means that it's all hands on deck to help Barack Obama become the 44th President of the United States of America. Let's get to work.

25

We Have It in Our Power to Begin the World Over Again

o o o o o o o o o o o o o o o o o o o o o o o o o o o o o

Keith Ferguson writes a weekly editorial blog for Barack the Youth Vote. He is a 2005 graduate of the University of Puget Sound, where he studied English and History. Originally a native of Colorado Springs, Colorado, Keith currently lives in New York City.

Moments when I feel—truly feel—that distinct essence of being an American:

- singing "Take Me Out to the Ball Game" during the 7th inning stretch
- stopping at a gas station on a cross-country road trip
- watching fireworks on the Fourth of July
- listening to Ray Charles' version of "America the Beautiful"
- wearing old blue jeans and sneakers while mowing the lawn

It's quite a portrait, is it not? In fact, I might even say that these experiences are almost like virtual snapshots of modern America; taken together, you find a collage of what happens from day-to-day between these oceans that encapsulate us. It's all there: the baseball, the open road, the freedom, the rhythm and blues, and of course, the blue jeans.

But these are moments when you expect to feel American. They are synonymous with American living. And even though we all have our own unique experiences of these moments, with our own friends and families, the fact remains that we, as a people, share them. They are what make this land your land, as well as my land.

I think that in order to actually get down to the business of truly discovering the essence of being an American however, you have to come across a few moments that you never could have expected; moments that are on their surface not characteristically or definitively American at all, at least not in any typical, star-spangled kind of way. That's my story at least.

In addition to the handful of experiences listed above, there is another group that has made me realize, on a more personal level, what it means to be an American. They are perhaps less obvious than baseball and fireworks, but the truth is, they have informed what I believe most about my role as an American citizen. This is not a complete list, for sure, but it begins to get at what being an American means to me and what I believe 2008 could mean for America.

The first four of these five moments are:

- listening to "Revolution" by the Beatles for the first time

- re-reading Thomas Paine's *Common Sense* and actually understanding it

- hearing Pulitzer-prize winning journalist David Halberstam's answer to my question

- interviewing my classmate for a documentary film

REVOLUTION

You know the song. Paul kicks the whole thing off with an inspired, raw yowl right before the distorted guitars crash down on all of us. And then there is John singing about changing the world, his lips snarled in determination. At times, in the archival footage of this recording, he even looks so enraged he could drop the guitar and start a fight. It's incredible, actually. You don't even have to understand the words of this song to know it means business. This song is big, tough, and a little off its rocker. You get the sense that if this song was a kid on the playground, it would be beating up all the other songs.

And it's because this song communicates the danger and anger of revolution.

This song succeeded where every textbook I read in school as a child failed: it gave me a sense of what revolution felt like—the danger and anger—and it gave me an idea of what the American revolutionists must have felt. This was how I began to humanize the colonists who dared to imagine the world in an entirely new way and how I began to understand the truly radical nature of their ideas of liberty and equality. Patrick Henry didn't have distorted guitars, but with lyrics like "Give me liberty or give me death" maybe he didn't need them.

A WORLD OF PAINE

I could have used a catchy melody the first time I crossed paths with Thomas Paine. The summer before my junior year of high school, I had a lot of reading to do in preparation for my AP U.S. History class. In addition to reading the first third of our class textbook and maintaining a meticulous reading log, I also was expected to independently study the primary sources of a Founder of my choice. I chose Thomas Paine, and as I spent the last day of that summer alone in my bedroom reading (but not absorbing) his *Common Sense*, I found myself thinking: "This guy stirred the people to revolt with this long-winded babble? How?" That is to say, I didn't get it. And with less than 24 hours until the first day of school, I didn't really have time to try.

Which is a shame. *Common Sense* is timeless, but only if you take the time to understand it.

For me, that came years later, when I came across this passage: "We have it in our power to begin the world over again." Huh, I wondered. Which John Lennon song is that from? Turns out, it's from a little revolutionary pamphlet called *Common Sense*. And just as I found it so stirring and compelling at the turn of the 20th century, so did the American revolutionaries in the 18th century. Because of these words and the actions they inspired, the world as the colonists and everyone else knew it, truly did begin over again.

And then, as I re-read on, it was as if Paine knew that one summer day in my teens, his common sense would be way over my head when he wrote, "When we are planning for posterity, we ought to remember that virtue is not hereditary." What I realized when I re-read this passage later was that the new world Paine helped create, the one I enjoyed, was dependent on American posterity understanding the very virtue of that new world.

That world was America. That posterity was me. And it was time I discovered the virtue at the heart of this truth.

BEST AND BRIGHTEST

I was fortunate to enjoy a dinner with David Halberstam, the famous journalist renowned for his coverage of Vietnam, in the fall of 2003. He visited my alma mater, the University of Puget Sound, to lecture on his book, *The Children*. A small group of faculty and students were invited to meet Mr. Halberstam to discuss the issues of the day with him the night before his lecture. The dinner conversation primarily focused on the war in Iraq, imbedded journalism, and the Bush administration—and what all of these had in common with Vietnam. I left the dinner with so many thoughts and questions that I did not know where to begin unpacking them.

The next night, when Mr. Halberstam took questions from the audience after his lecture, I stood and asked him this: What is the role of politicians in leading the nation in confronting some of the more painful aspects of our history? He responded that the answers lay in reading; in our leaders' curiosity in and knowledge of the world. Only in this way will leaders know where they are leading from historically and be able to help the nation address the difficulties of our past.

Standing there, addressing a man whose influence shaped the history of his times, I felt the wisdom of his words. Since hearing them, I have increasingly felt that the best hopes for our future lay in our true understanding of our past. If those of us inheriting this nation's wounds could take it upon ourselves to look to our past and begin to find their remedies, indeed this generation might earn that title made famous by Mr. Halberstam: the best and the brightest.

WE GENERATION

My interest and faith in my generation led me to initiate a film project my senior year of college. In lieu of writing a term paper for my final U.S. History course, "The United States in the 1960s," I partnered with a classmate and undertook a documentary that addressed the question of what the legacy of this period—a half-century past—meant for the next American generation.

Fourteen members of the class participated in one-on-one interviews, where we discussed broad themes from the 1960s: the civil rights movements, the fight for liberation, the birth of the modern political spectrum, the war in Vietnam, and the idea of generational identity. It was here, on this idea of a generational identity, that the ultimate question was addressed: what does this past have to do with our future?

The responses of my classmates were incredibly intriguing. I ultimately found a group of people who believed our generation was capable of tremendous good, even acknowledging that we had been thus far somewhat slow in making an impact on our times. It was as if, somewhat nervously, a belief in ourselves as a generation was bubbling beneath the surface.

And it finally peaked through in the words of one of my classmates who said that he just simply but truly believed in us—this generation. He did not care about what divided us, because he believed that we would recognize all that we stood to gain by realizing what united us. We, we, we—he kept saying the word over and over again. And it made something in me click. After devoting weeks to talking with these young Americans about the legacy of the 1960s, I realized this: the answer to the Me Generation was going to be the We Generation. And the idea of being part of that inspired me. The bubbling beneath the surface is real and we finally have a reason to let it flow forth.

This brings me to the fifth and final moment that brought me to a discovery of what it means to be an American.

THE AUDACITY OF HOPE

The summer of 2004 was an anxious time for those of us who believed that the country needed new leadership, that the very foundational principles of the republic were jeopardized without the intervention of a new direction. John Kerry was our man and the Democratic National Convention in Boston was his moment to rally the people to this cause. And I really thought that ultimately, come November, people would be rallied.

Even as someone who entered the week of the convention with a great degree of enthusiasm, ready to vote for Kerry and stump for Kerry, I never expected to be so honestly and completely stirred and energized … but not by Kerry; by a state senator from Illinois whom I had never heard of.

Out of nowhere, came Barack Obama saying what I thought! What I knew was true! What I had never heard any leader say in my lifetime!

He began with his own story, speaking of his modest roots as the son of a goat herder and the grandson of a cook. He told his story, one of dreams and ambition, and emphasized how his experience was the realization of the American promise. His story was part of the American story. And the greatness of his own life's journey reminded me of the greatness of America's promise.

Obama spoke of America at its best: as tolerant and generous. He made clear that the American tradition was to constantly seek to grow in each of these founding virtues. It is why he owes a debt to his forbearers; it is why we all owe a debt to our forbearers. When we do so, Obama said, we affirm the greatness of this nation.

I felt proud of America and being an American. Obama had barely been on stage five minutes and he had reminded me of the simplicity and the decency of America's primary purpose. I felt called anew to serve that purpose. "Our pride," Obama said, "is based on a very simple premise, summed up in a declaration made over two hundred years ago, 'We hold these truths to he self-evident, that all men are created equal. That they are endowed by their Creator with certain inalienable rights. That among these are life, liberty and the pursuit of happiness.'" Hearing these familiar words from the Declaration of Independence again, this time from Obama, I felt a reverence for these words as I never had before.

He reminded me that these words are what bind all Americans to one another. By them, we are able to do well by one another. The idea of America as a community, invested in the interests of one another was a de-emphasized notion in 2004. We were then a people that reflected our politics: deliberately and passionately divided. How compelling it was to reflect on the common ground that we truly shared as a people, starting with the inspired words of the Declaration of Independence. Building on that notion, Obama said this, which I will never forget and which I will always keep close to my heart:

> "There are those who are preparing to divide us, the spin masters and negative ad peddlers who embrace the politics of anything goes. Well, I say to them tonight, there's not a liberal America and a conservative America—there's the United States of America. There's not a black America and white America and Latino America and Asian America; there's the United States of America. The pundits like to slice-and-dice our country into Red States and Blue States; Red States for Republicans, Blue States for Democrats. But I've got news for them, too. We worship an awesome God in the Blue States, and we don't like federal agents poking around our libraries in the Red States. We coach Little League in the Blue States and have gay friends in the Red States. There are patriots who opposed the war in Iraq and patriots who supported it. We are one people, all of us pledging allegiance to the stars and stripes, all of us defending the United States of America."

In mere minutes, he summarized the foundational hopes of this nation—and he reminded me that those virtuous principles our Founders revolted for were being betrayed by the politics of my time. The reason I knew this to be true was because even I, despite my excitement over the convention, had not actually expected to be so compelled by it; yet, this moment of authentic inspiration generated by Obama revealed how small my expectations of my leaders, my fellow citizens, and even myself truly were.

I realized that it was possible to expect more. And what I have learned since is that it is my duty to expect more: of my leaders, of my fellow citizens, and of myself. I now find Obama's presidential candidacy so urgent and important for the nation because he believes this too, and he does expect more of himself as a leader. I see examples of this in his refusal to accept the money of lobbyists to fuel his campaign and also in his prescience and new vision concerning the war in Iraq. He also expects more of us as citizens, as he calls all of us to take part in this campaign and begin looking to our history for wisdom and direction in our own communities. Because he appreciates the best of our nation's past, I believe he is ready to lead us to the best of our nation's future.

This personal realization, brought on by a man who simply recited the opening of the Declaration of Independence and embodied its promise, is the most important moment I've yet experienced in discovering what it means to be an American.

I say this because the words of the Declaration of Independence are the words born of revolutionary virtue; they are the words that began the world over again; they are the words that will heal our collective past in their very fulfillment; because these are the words that will unite our generation to reclaim the American dream; and because these are the words evoked so sincerely by this new leader who has already given name to that defining cause of our time: the audacity of hope.

In the midst of discovering what being an American means to me, I believe that the meaning of the 2008 election stands to mean the rediscovery of common sense for this country. And I believe that the next American generation will be leading the way, supporting Barack Obama and acting in understanding of Paine's words: "Tis not the concern of a day, a year, or an age; posterity are virtually involved in the contest, and will be more or less affected, even to the end of time, by the proceedings now. Now is the seed time of continental union, faith and honor."

"And if you will join me in this improbable quest, if you feel destiny calling, and see as I see, a future of endless possibility stretching before us; if you sense, as I sense, that the time is now to shake off our slumber, and slough off our fear, and make good on the debt we owe past and future generations, then I'm ready to take up the cause, and march with you, and work with you. Together, starting today, let us finish the work that needs to be done, and usher in a new birth of freedom on this Earth."

—Barack Obama, Feb. 10, 2007, Springfield, Illinois

978-0-595-46703-7
0-595-46703-2

Printed in the United States
110815LV00004B/196/A